Some reviews for 'Th

'It is very many yea
at the funny parts of a
completely in agreeme … message.

'Please accept my heartiest congratulations . . . '

'Your book deserves a record sale'

'Your book will do more to teach our people about the importance of a Navy than all the preaching I have been trying to do since 1938.'

'Congratulations on a stunning book.'

Some extracts from an extensive letter to the author from Dr. John De Courcy Ireland, this country's leading authority on all aspects of maritime matters, who has been decorated by many Governments throughout the world for his distinguished work into maritime history.

'The service can be stifling within the lower ranks, and "The Irish Navy — What a Life!" shows just what life was like for those who had none of the benefits of officer rank.'
— *Afloat Magazine*

'Mr Brady's description of Navy life reminds us of the conditions in one of the worst places where a man could find work.'

'The whole is described in a cheerful narrative style and is great fun to read and very believable.'

'At the end of the book is a good assessment of the Navy to-day, and praise for the vessels they run, and the huge improvements for the men and the present day professionalism of the officers.'

'Anyone with an interest in Ireland and the sea will be delighted with this book.'
— *The Irish Skipper*

'Some of the descriptions come with strong language, but the book is a lively amusing account of life at sea in the lower ranks.'

— *Marine Times'*

'Very funny and provocative.'
— *R.T.E. Radio One*

'A great and amusing insight'
'Select Bibliography, Ireland Country Profile,'
The Economist Intelligence Unit, London 1997.

THE IRISH NAVY
What a Life!

Hilarious Tales from Below Deck

Jim Brady

Anchor Press

First published in 1996
Corrected, revised and updated in 2002
by Anchor Press

5 Ballinteer Grove
Dublin 16

ISBN 0 9528447 3 7

Cover illustration by Philip Gray
Riverside Art, Cork Dockyard, Rushbrooke,
Cobh, Co. Cork.

Colour separations and scanning
by Typeform Repro
Portside Business Centre, Dublin.

Typesetting, origination and page assembly by
The Red Setter, Dublin.

Printed by Betaprint, Dublin.

Contents

Dedication,

To all serving personnel, and former officers, NCO's and men of the Naval Service, for their devotion to duty in the security of this State be forever remembered.

CREDITS

Author's Notes

This is not a serious history of the Naval Service, that has been successfully completed by others.

This is a humourous account of (barrack-room, below-deck) life, and to present an authentic view of everyday activity within the ranks, I was compelled to use names of real people, some of whom have passed on, most are happily still with us and a few are actually still serving in the Naval Service.

In this narrative I have presented the human strengths and weaknesses of many of my former colleagues, and by doing so, I do not wish this to be conveyed as criticism, since I continue to regard them as comrades. The criticism is reserved for myself.

Special Thanks

A very special word of thanks to Nuala Gunn (The Red Setter) who tragically died while typesetting the final stages of this book.

To G. W. Rushbrooke for your invaluable and consistent help and support, and Loraine for your encouragement. Thanks also to Philip Gray, professional artist and former Naval Service Petty Officer for the cover illustration, and Paddy Burns and Patrick Boland for your patience and most helpful advice and assistance.
Thanks Sandra for your efficient typing.

Joining Up

I was an uneducated and unemployed 15 year old boy living in a huge Corporation housing complex with absolutely no future prospects. But then the talk on the road was that some of my older school pals had either joined the British Army, or the Royal Navy, and had, on their home leave told everyone how great it was being in the forces, the great money they were earning, the lovely rooms they lived in, the smashing food they were served up in the attractive dining halls, and above all, the women they were able to pull because they looked great in their brilliant uniforms which were also provided free of charge.

After hearing all that, I immediately decided that this was the life for me. The only problem was that you must be 18 and show a birth certificate. I was only 15 and it was very hard at that age to forge one of those. So for months, I worked my immature brain as to how to overcome this problem. But then one night, my father brought home the Dublin *Evening Herald* and there on page three was an advert looking for young and strong able bodied men for the army and navy. It also published a picture showing an army private, and a naval rating walking down the street in their number one uniforms, and looking very smart. So, there and then I made up my mind to enlist without delay. Just think, I said to myself, my own room and bed, and maybe a radio to keep me company. Perhaps a nice carpet beside the bed in case I need to get up at night. Good pay and a nice uniform to go out at night to chat up the women, and then take them to a select lounge bar. I could maybe stay the night, and then ramble back to base the following morning for a rest, after a good warm breakfast. The possibilities were endless. They might make me an officer after a couple of months. I could even command my own warship, and end my days as a highly respected admiral. Yes, this definitely is the life for me. Just think of how things were going to be. I couldn't sleep that night, tossing and turning, and dreaming of life on the ocean wave, rushing from one foreign port to another. Bermuda, Miami, the China Seas, or even Japan, and then return to the Irish coastal waters for the summer patrols and a little holiday with my parents. Oh yes, life is going to be great!

So, bright and early the following morning, I rushed down to the nearest army Barracks, Clancy in Islandbridge and told the soldier on the gate that I was willing to join the navy because I wanted to see the world as soon as possible. "How old are you?" "15". "Fuck Off". "But I am willing to serve and be sent to Cork and sail on a ship." "Go home to your mother son,you are still wet behind the ears, and come back when you are 17, and bring written permission from your father to join." "But there must be some mistake. Last night's *Herald* said the navy wants recruits urgently, because they must have bought brand new ships". "If you don't get away from here, I will give you a kick up the arse. Go back up to Ballyfermot, you gobshite".

I went home to my mother half crying after being rejected for active service. "What happened?" she said. "They wouldn't take me because I hadn't written permission from my father. "Don't worry, I will ask him as soon as he has his dinner". He eventually arrived home on his bicycle at ten, half drunk as usual. (He worked in a wine and spirit importers, and it seems he drank most of it). "Dad", I said, "will you write out a note saying it's alright for me to join the navy? They want me to go on a ship at Haulbowline immediately". "OK son, but be careful of the women on the quay walls". He of course meant the docks around New York or San Francisco. "I'll be careful Dad, I know what they're like". He nearly fell off his chair. It was of course all that whiskey inside him. The next day I cycled down to Collins Barracks for an interview with the Commanding Officer. The PA Corporal at the gate stopped me and asked what I wanted. I informed him that I was reporting for sea duty, and could I see the man in charge. "How old are you?" "Seventeen and a half" "Take that twit up to the Recruiting Office, he ordered another soldier. Inside the so-called office, were two chairs and a table, and of course the inevitable turf-burning fire. The place was filthy, and in fact, smelt like the bog. In marched a scruffy small and fat red faced sergeant smoking a woodbine butt and smelling of Guinness. "What do you want?" "I'm going to join the Navy". "Where's the permission from your father?" "Here". "He must have written that when he was drunk, or did you scribble it out?" "No, sir". "I'm a Sergeant, not a fucking Officer. Why don't you go into the army?" "I hate that green suit that they wear, and I want to see the world". "Listen, you fucking eejit, you are going to the arsehole of Ireland, and that's as far as you'll go". He is just jealous I thought, stuck here in a crumbling old barracks with no prospects of ever seeing overseas service. Look at the state of this room. Sure it's only fit for pigs and the state of his army boots, with hob-nails and all, and the uniform, it's made up of bull's wool. I can't wait until I get into the navy. I'll have my own room, own washing facilities, own private toilet, and maybe even a wardrobe to hang my officer's uniform as soon as I get it.

"You have to pass a stiff medical examination to get into this man's outfit" he said, "and if our doctor finds as much as a flaw on your body, you won't be let in and that's it. "OK where is he? I'm perfect, and there's not a mark on me". "Come back at 4". The doctor on seeing me said drop your trousers, bend down, and then he held my private parts with both his hands and said "cough, cough again, and again". I thought to myself, what's bending down and touching your toes with a man standing behind you, then holding your testicles, and asking a stupid question like "cough" got to do with the Navy? My only summary was that it could be an all male club with no women ever allowed aboard ship. It doesn't matter, it can't be perfect, sure there are still the foreign ports to look forward to, and all the lovely girls. "You are in perfect physical condition Brady, and ideally suited to serve with your colleagues aboard ship." "Yes, sir," I answered smartly, "and thank you very much." "Sergeant", he ordered, "make out a travelling warrant for this man, he is enlisting in the Navy". At last, my dream has come true. I rushed for the 79 bus, and outside our corporation house, I jumped off, full of excitement to tell my mother the great news. "Mother", I said, "I can't wait for that stew, because I have to immediately report for sea duty. I'm catching the quarter to seven train to Cork, they want me in the Navy". "Well, here's some sandwiches" "I won't need them, I will be looked after when I reach Cork". "Which way is that?" she asked. I didn't repeat what the sergeant in the barracks had said. "I'm off, I'll send you a post card from the first port of call". "Good luck, son, and keep away from the women". The women, I thought, just wait until I get my hands on them, they will be sorry we Irish sailors ever left their home waters. I again ran for the bus which left me right outside the station, and when I entered, the clock stated ten minutes to six, and the place was completely deserted except for the porter. So I asked him what time was the next train to Cork. "6.45", he answered. "What's 6.45?" "A quarter to seven". It finally arrived at the platform and I immediately jumped on board and just couldn't wait until it finally moved right on time. The young and attractive nun who sat next to me asked if I would mind placing her large black leather suitcase next to my luggage on the rack overhead. I answered: "of course not". Only then did it occur to me that I had in fact absolutely no belongings with me except what I stood in, a long grey wool overcoat down to my ankles with a wide belt and very deep pockets with large flaps, a blue two-piece suit, that was two sizes too small, a pair of black leather boots, a grey coloured fluffy scarf, and a blue shirt and tie. My mother had bought that lot from a friend in the Iveagh Secondhand clothes market for 12 shillings and sixpence and she had only retrieved my overcoat and suit from the pawnbroker in James's Street the previous Saturday morning so that I could, along with herself and my father, attend mass in the new church in Ballyfermot. All I possessed was a ten shilling note I got from my father, and I wasn't breaking that. That cash was for my first big night out on the town when I arrive. I took very little notice of the others on the train, but I did notice that there was a large number of nuns and priests on board (also perhaps travelling on travelling warrants) and children running along the carriages and the waiter carrying lovely smelling hot food, presumably up to the first class passengers. It was very dark outside, and it was raining, but I did observe very clearly the familiar sight of the houses in Ballyfermot nearby, as we travelled smoothly along the tracks. I do, however, clearly remember stopping at the dreary looking stations of Portlaoise and Limerick Junction, but the remainder of the journey is now just a blur, because I was simply so excited and couldn't wait for the end of the trip. I finally did arrive in Cork at about 10.30 and nobody was there to welcome me. "Where's everybody?" I thought. All I saw were the passengers getting off the train, and heading in all directions with strange sounding accents. "Where's the Navy?" I asked a man dressed in brown overalls. "You've got to get another train", he replied, "and it doesn't leave until 11.20!"

I was starving and freezing cold, so I very reluctantly decided to break my ten shillings so I went into the station tearooms and bought a cup of tea. The stuff looked like and tasted like ink, but at least it was hot! Never mind I reminded myself, good quality food is just a few miles away. I made my way to the train, and the arrow pointing to it said Cobh. I never heard of that place, I wonder what it looks like? They told me I was going to Cork, so I looked at my ticket does it say Cork or Cobh?They were expecting me, and I was sure they had everything ready for my imminent arrival. So just to be on the safe side, I purchased a one way ticket to Cobh. That's another two shillings gone from my ten bob. But it doesn't matter, the money is great down here, and I might be able to perhaps send a fiver a week back home from whatever country I might visit. Yes life felt really good. I stepped on to a freezing cold steam locomotive driven train, and the carriages were from the Victorian age. The seats were as hard as wood, and the padding inside was lumpy. I immediately started scratching my legs, and my lower back. Then I suddenly realised to my horror that the seats were walking with fleas. It moved off on time, and stopped to pick up and unload passengers at Little Island, Cobh Junction, Fota, Carragaloe, Rushbrooke, and finally Cobh itself, and still there was no reception committee. Surely there must be some terrible mistake? They knew I was coming down so perhaps they were told the wrong time?

Anyway, I followed the other passengers straight up Cobh from the station and after a while I decided to look for the Naval Base. Then all of a sudden, the thundering sound of the Cathedral bells rang out twelve times. It was midnight on Friday January 27th, 1956, then all the lights in the town immediately went out. I was totally alone freezing cold, frightened, starving and lost in a very strange place. I again started wandering about, and approximately five minutes later a young sailor in uniform emerged from behind a wall close to Andy's Well House public bar, and following close behind a young woman looking rather the worst for wear. Well I did remember hearing somewhere that every girl loves a sailor. I asked him for directions to the Naval Station, and he replied that he was just returning there for the night. He kissed her goodnight and promised her he would contact her again very soon. He then said we better hurry because the Navy's launch leaves in a few minutes. On the way down to the pier I told him that I thought I heard other voices back close to Andy's where I met him. He burst out laughing and explained that on the previous Saturday night, he and four of his shipmates went up to Cork. They had a few drinks and then went to a dance in the Arcadia where they shifted a few birds. The women agreed to meet them here in Cobh, and they had earlier in the day arrived together by train from Cork. "They are staying here overnight at the Westbourne B&B where I'm staying with her tomorrow night because I have to report back tonight". "But where are the others?" I asked. "Ah, they're down further near the Ormonde Cinema. There wasn't enough room for the rest of them where I was". "Yes", I murmured to myself, "this is definitely the place for me!" We reached the pier just as the boat was pulling out and we both jumped on board. I had almost missed my destiny!

On board my immediate impression was that everyone there were very young, spotlessly clean and most were in the uniform similar to which I had seen in the *Evening Herald*. Some had much drink taken. Everyone knew one another, and the topic of conversation was naturally the young girls ashore, and oddly I thought their duties allocated to them for the following morning. They somehow were proud to be discussing that point, and were rather looking forward to the next day's work. I was soon to find out what that involved. My second observation was that nearly everybody was tagged with a nickname. The Blusher was mentioned while he was out of earshot. He was a fine chap who was very unlucky to have been born with a severe birthmark right down the left side of his entire body. Another lad was referred to as Almost because they felt he was almost human, and of course the usual names of Spud, Sparks, Chippy, and Nobby Clarke.

Then they turned their full attention to me, the new recruit, and right away asked me where did I get my suit and overcoat. "In Burtons in Dublin of course", I answered shyly. "More like off the knackers", answered Meehan sharply. Almost said: "I bet you sixpence his grandfather died and left it to him". "No", Hano said, "it's too old for that". So the slagging went on and on, until Benny Cullen brought my attention to a sign that read Submarine Cables, and he tried to convince me that our navy had submarines. I didn't know what ships we possessed, but I was almost certain we didn't have subs. The sign is still there and it simply means that there are submerged electric cables in the locality. After a fifteen minute journey we arrived at the Naval Base at Haulbowline Island in Cork Harbour, where my life was about to change utterly. Literally overnight, I was to change from a boy into a man, and my great expectations were also to change dramatically.

The Welcoming Committee

Most of us stepped ashore, while those who remained on board which included army personnel and their families continued around Haulbowline Island to the military establishment of Spike Island. When I reached the top steps of the wharf I was immediately stopped by two naval men in uniform, whom I later identified as the Duty Officer, and the duty Petty Officer. They inquired as to who I was, and where I thought I was going. I answered as smartly as possible, because now I was part of the military machine, that I was their new man that they were expecting. So I demanded as firmly as I could as to where my quarters were, and where I could have my meal, since I had not eaten since early morning way back in Dublin. They then looked at one another for at least five seconds, and the officer asked me for my identification. I asked them: "what's that?" "Have you any ID?" "What?" "Who are you?" "Jim Brady", I answered. "We know nothing about you, go home". "I can't, I've only got six shillings left out of ten bob". The officer then ordered the PO to call out the guard from the guard room and have me escorted there for the night.

After about ten minutes two young sailors arrived and marched me off to the guardroom. When I entered that jailhouse, I was instantly handed over to a man who they called the "Commander". I knew very little about naval ranks or insignia at that stage, but I was quite sure that he was no commander, because he neither spoke like one, acted like one, or looked like one. He was dressed similar to the others with a sailor's hat with a silk ribbon and tassel, and a heavy dark wool blue two piece suit, with bell-bottom trousers. He also wore a canvas belt with a well polished brass buckle with two pouches which held spare bullets for their rifles. He also wore canvas leggings tucked into his trousers, and a very heavy pair of brown army boots which had been partly dyed black to match his uniform. Both his belt and leggings had been whitened with a water based whitening, because that mixture was running down the uniforms of the others who had just brought me in from the rain. I recognised that whitening because my mother used to paste it onto our canvas runners every Sunday in the summer before she took us for the day trip to the sea at Sandymount.

The only difference I could find between the crew of the jail was that the "Commander" wore a very thin gold stripe on his right arm, and the others kept calling him "Ellis". So, I assumed his name was Ellis. Therefore, I referred to him by that name. He then very angrily told me that his name was LS (Leading Seaman — sounds like Ellis), Gene O'Shea Guard Commander. (I later found out that he also kept pigs ashore because he used to collect the swill from the naval cookhouses). "I see" I said, and then I sat down at the small coal burning fire that was boiling a large pot of tea. After a few minutes they removed from one of the cells a kit bag containing a big package which was wrapped in grease proof paper. Inside the wrapping was about three pounds of butter. (I had never seen that amount before, we were reared on stork margarine). Also included was about the same weight of big German sausages and streaky rashers, a brown paper bag of eggs, and four large white loaves. I said to myself some of those goodies must be for me because they will never shift that lot. So I politely, asked the "Commander" for a bit of a fry-up since I hadn't eaten all day. He and the other jailers told me to fuck off because that was their rations for the entire night. After a while they relented and offered me a large mug of tea and a bully beef sandwich, and after devouring that morsel in one go, I fell onto one of the beds in the cell and immediately fell into a deep coma type sleep, completely exhausted after a very exciting and eventful day.

The Food & Accommodation

I was disturbed from my dream of commanding my own vessel by the duty PO who was standing over me. "Brady" he said, "we found your papers in the ship's office (main base office), and the writers (pen pushers) forgot to tell us about you and that's why you weren't brought across from Cobh by the shore patrol". So much for the reception committee! "Am I not wanted then?" I asked. Nobody answered. "Come on" the PO said, "and we'll find you a bunk somewhere for the night". "But I thought I would have my own private room". "You fucking smart arse Dublin jackeen red arses are all the same", he replied. Things were going drastically wrong for me, I could feel it in my bones. He brought me down to a prehistoric looking two storey building, which had an ugly clock that didn't work (and still doesn't) fitted into it, but he politely named it the main billets. Inside was packed about two hundred new recruits like myself all asleep. This dormitory type structure was divided in two by a plywood partition and each bed was separated by about six feet and all beds were lined up in rows and facing one another. A small bulb was left lighting all night and, according to him it was called a pilot light, to guide those who may need to get up during the night. This "accommodation" definitely did not suit my purpose. After a short while he found a vacant bunk for me between two very country looking young fellas with red faces and buck teeth and both were snoring very heavily. Two heavy grey army blankets with two FF stamps on both of them, and a hard and lumpy pillow was lying close by covered with cigarette ash and fluff from the blankets on all the beds nearby. "Surely, PO, you don't expect me to sleep here in that filthy so-called bed, surrounded by strangers, who I never saw before? Anyway, how can I sleep with that crowd of culchies snoring like pigs?" "Just get into it and shut your mouth or I'll lock you up in the guardroom for the night, and bring you before the CO first thing in the morning.

Eventually I got into the so-called bed, fully clothed and again immediately fell fast asleep. It must have been all that sea air. The following morning, I suddenly awoke to the most annoying voice I have ever heard in my short life. It was the sound of an untrained voice shouting through a loudhailer, "call the hands", "call the hands", over and over again. I must be having a nightmare I thought, so I simply turned over and pulled my warm overcoat up around my shoulders. Suddenly the dreaded PO burst through the door shouting "Get up you lousy crowd of fuckers", while kicking all the beds with his heavy dyed black boots, and rattling them with his large cane walking stick. I must be in hell, I whispered to myself, but then all the other recruits (red arses) jumped from their beds without question and commenced removing their towels which were all stencil stamped with large numbers in black ink and running through the towels were the green, white and orange colours of the Irish Republic's flag.

It was still dark so I asked "What time is it?" Someone answered: "7 o'clock". "And where are you all going?" "To the washhouse to get ready and then down for breakfast". "What time is that at?" I asked. "8 o'clock". "Ah well there's plenty of time, I'll just wait here until about ten to eight". The PO again returned to the billet and ordered me out of the bed. "Oh God", I thought, "what have I got myself into?" I eventually dragged my weary body out of the contraption they called a bunk and followed the others into the washhouse and toilets which were situated at the centre of the building. The smell of course was terrible, with so many in turn using the six toilets which were fitted, and the large urinal which was the complete length of the wall and that was overflowing because the filter was stuffed with bits of soap and cigarette butts. I waited unable to decide what to do. Then a six foot three lad about two years my senior approached me and offered me the use of his towel and soap. From that moment a close friendship was to last until he passed away nearly thirty years later. Joe "Stretch" Lynch then had the worst haircut and hairstyle I have ever seen before or since. All the hair on top of his head was standing up straight and spiky just like a hedgehog's, and the hair on the side and back was gappy, and in places it was cut so tight that the skin was actually torn and a trickle of blood was running. Very soon I was to be introduced to the naval barber who was responsible for this butchery. The others also wore similar hairstyles, but none were quite so bad. Perhaps Joe "Stretch" visited the "barber" on a bad day?

Anyway I washed quickly while some of the others were attempting to shave with safety razors. A few were succeeding, but it was difficult because most had no hair on their faces, and it was dangerous using a razor on skin covered in pimples. A few on the other side of the partition were showering while the hot water lasted, when suddenly a great deal of commotion developed because a new and very shy young fella wouldn't take off his shorts in front of the others. So then the slagging started. A Kerry fella said, "why are you afraid to show it, is it too small, and are you ashamed?" "No", said Hector, it's too big!" Paddy Smith said: "you are both dead wrong, because he's only showing it to his girlfriend ashore". "Doyler" wondered if he had one at all. Frank Thunder who was later to become a marathon poker player on the ships, suddenly pulled down the woollen shorts from the bashful young sailor, and revealed to all that in fact it was only normal in size and shape. (I was now ageing very rapidly). Anyway, after all the fun and confusion, that revelation was literally a let down for all concerned. We returned to the billet and the other occupants immediately commenced making up their beds, and polishing their boots and shoes. Then I learnt the proper way to make up a bed military style, but not my own because that still was only a heap of scrap.

Firstly you strip the bed completely, then you place one blanket over the mattress and tuck in all the loose ends. Then you fold up four times two more blankets and your two sheets making sure that their blue lines are facing out. Then you place your pillow on the foot of the bed, place one blanket over that, then a sheet, another blanket, and the other sheet. You fold your remaining blanket in half and wrap it around everything. The bed now looks rather neat and tidy.

Suddenly the same untrained and annoying voice that had disturbed my sleep earlier, screamed over the loud hailer again, ordering everyone to breakfast. I said to myself: "I'm in the wrong place, this all sounds like Mountjoy Prison". Then, just as we all left for my first real meal, somebody, completely off key started blowing a whistle over the same loudhailer. (I later identified it as a Boatswain's pipe). Immediately, everyone stood stiffly to attention, and I said: "what in heaven's name is going on in this place?" "Look up to the Square (Parade Ground)" Joe "Stretch" said,"they are hoisting up the flag". Sure enough, there were the Duty Officer and PO whom I had met on my arrival the night before finishing their twenty-four hour shift. After a moment, we continued down to the ratings dining hall. Inside the floor was packed with young lads all talking together. They were eating off formica topped tables, and sitting on long, rough wooden benches. I followed "Stretch" into the cookhouse to collect the food which was handed out through a wooden hatch. Inside was a chap dressed like a chef, standing over a very long coal fired cooker and oven. The breakfast, if it could be called that, consisted of burned black pudding, similar to the buttons that are fitted to a black waterproof overcoat; an egg, also burned to a crisp and two black sausages. A heel of white bread with a slice of butter melting into it was also handed out. "Doyler" loaned me his enamel mug to go inside to the kitchen to drain some tea from the boiler. On my way back to our table, I noticed that another young man was almost hidden behind a huge pile of dirty dishes, and the sink he was behind was overflowing with soapy water and bits of uneaten food because he never bothered to remove it before he steeped them.

When I returned, "Doyler" and "Stretch" explained that the guy inside was the duty messman and his name was Arthur English, or "Ingo". Much later on, Mr "Ingo" was to have a major bearing on my life. As I tried desperately to chew my black pudding, I asked the others was the food for real. They replied: "of course, this is great compared to what we were dished out yesterday morning. It was a kipper lying in cold water on its own, full of small bones, which we also ate, because we were so hungry". "Hector" interrupted and remarked that he actually drank the water and would have scraped off the FF from the plate he was so hungry. I of course, didn't believe a word of it.

Later that morning I was to find out how they actually managed to prevent themselves from starving to death. However, after about twenty minutes, I managed to cut up into small and manageable pieces the "food" they provided and then swallowed the portions with the help of plenty of tea which I later discovered was laced with brown colouring from a bottle to make it appear strong. We eventually returned back to the billet and to my great surprise, the occupants were cleaning and polishing everything. It was the Commanding Officer's Rounds day. Therefore, there was no other work to be done, and when the place was all cleared up, the ratings off duty had the weekend free to themselves. That, I discovered was why everybody on the launch the previous night was in such good form. The NCO in charge of the billet then ordered O'Flaherty from Galway to collect the lead swinger from next door and clean his room, which was at the far end of the billet. The lead swinger is an ugly piece of equipment with a wooden handle and about ten pounds of lead attached to it, and a piece of a worn army blanket wrapped around it. It's used to polish lino which has been waxed, and the NCO was blessed with his own room and a piece of green lino, his only comfort.

I commenced tidying up, but he then said to me "Brady, you've to see the 'Doc' down at the hospital".

I, politely as I could answered that I was medically examined in Dublin's Collins Barracks only yesterday and that I was perfectly fit. "Get fucking down", he said, "or I'll throw you out of that window". "Yes, PO", I replied. "Stretch" volunteered to escort me down to the hospital. We passed the so-called cookhouse and marched through the gate beside the jail house and headed straight down until we approached another grey and ancient building with "Hospital" written over it. We entered through two outer doors and then "Stretch" knocked on another door and the voice inside said "Come in!" Inside, sitting behind a table with an old telephone on it, and some sticking plaster with a bottle of some form of stomach mixture was a youngster around my age in a sailor's uniform, which had a red cross badge sewn on its left arm. "Stretch" Lynch referred to him as "Doc" and he didn't mind. In fact, he expected to be called that. I wondered what sort of place this was. He certainly was no doctor, that's for sure. First of all, he was too young, and he didn't wear a white coat. Anyway, this sure was no hospital.

So I asked could I use the toilet as an excuse to further investigate the place. There were definitely no wards or patients there. In fact, there was no medical equipment anywhere, just rooms with sinks fitted, and one had a bath, with odds and ends thrown around, although I did notice a few dark canvas stretchers with wooden handles. That lucky find was to be extremely useful to me at a later stage. I finally arrived back to the "Docs" consulting room, and he asked me what kept me. I replied that I had the runs and that the Bully beef sandwich in the guard room the night before must have been the cause of it. "Never eat kosher out of tins", he said, "it will run the guts out of you". "Thanks Doc , I said smiling. He then took a deck of cards out of the drawer, so I imagined that we were about to play a game of cards perhaps twenty-one or poker. He handed me one and asked "what's that?" I said "a card Doc". "No you fucking eejit, what number is written on it?" I held it for several seconds examining it, because it was printed with a range of different colours. "I think it's an eight". "Here, what's the number of that one, three is it? And this, a seven? All right", he agreed, "you've passed the colour blind test. Go back to your billet, you're fit for sea duty.

I wondered what he meant, so outside I asked a group of strangers what was a colour blind test for in the service. An able-seaman confidently answered that you must be able to identify all colours on lookout watch while at sea in order to report to the officer on duty the various colours associated with other ships, lighthouses, and marker buoys. "It's all to do with safety at sea, simple rules of the road, you see". I thanked him for that mouthful of important information and Joe Stretch remarked to me how well trained he was, but he added that he was an A/B, an able-bodied man.

We both marched back up through the naval base, and as we entered the billet the NCO roared at us and said "Get the fuck out of here, the CO is on his way up".

"I know where to go", said "Stretch". "We'll ramble down to the civvy canteen for a feed because ours is also being cleaned up for COs". We again marched down through the base with "Stretch" saluting everybody, and when we reached the canteen, hundreds of young sailors were already queuing up to be served. "This", he confessed, "is where we manage to stay alive", and he also revealed that the CO and his escort couldn't see us down here. "This is where we hide every Saturday morning". We joined the long queue and were finally served after about fifteen minutes. It was rather small inside with wooden topped tables and steel tubular chairs fitted to accommodate approximately twenty personnel. Therefore, the vast majority of the hungry customers were devouring their food outside on the grass or placed on the window sills or simply eating out of their own hands. Anyway, by the time we reached the counter very little choice was available. All they could offer were squashed tomato or egg sandwiches or cheese cakes or heavy currant cakes which everyone referred to as depth charges, because of their heavy weight, and the awful effect they had on the stomach. In fact they took days to digest. The egg and tomato sandwiches didn't appeal to me at all because they reminded me of the condition ours were in when we arrived at the seaside when we were children, after travelling on two buses from Ballyfermot, and then walking a few miles to Sandymount. The only difference in these sandwiches was that the sand and margarine was missing. Since I had little choice, I ordered four depth charges, two cheese cakes, a kit kat and a mug of tea, and to hell with the consequences. I was starving, and I simply didn't care anymore. I was later to deeply regret that hasty decision, because for the following four days I suffered from a severe dose of diarrhoea. "Stretch" knew better and just asked for one of each and the mug of tea, then we both went outside and mixed with the others.

Right away, "Stretch" mentioned to me that some of them were off the ships, and since I couldn't detect any difference between any of them, I said "how can you tell?" "I can smell them", he replied. He was of course quite right, as I was to prove at a later date. What clearly stays in my mind is that everyone except the two of us, were smoking cigarettes, mostly brands such as Players Medium, Gold Flake, and Woodbines. Jack Brennan, who was later to become another close friend, was smoking the American brand, Lucky Strike, which was a very strong brand. He offered me one which I accepted, and that was my first taste of that very addictive weed. However, I managed, after many years to kick the habit, after going through a difficult struggle. After about half an hour, somebody said that COs inspection was over, so everyone dispersed and went their own separate ways.

"Doyler", "Stretch", Jack Brennan and myself headed back up to the billet, and while entering the main gate at the guardroom, "Stretch" again gave a smart salute. The man in uniform who "Stretch" had saluted, ordered him back and calmly explained to him that you only salute Commissioned Officers and that he was not one of them . "I am a Warrant Officer (the highest non-commissioned officer in the service). That man I was informed was one of the really true gentlemen of the service, and was highly respected by all concerned. His name was Nick Kennedy from Wexford, who was not related to, but was introduced to President J F Kennedy, when he visited Wexford in June 1963 to revisit his ancestral home near New Ross.

When we reached the billet and entered the room, the smell of washing soda, Jeyes fluid, polish, bleach and soap was overpowering, but at least I knew the place was clean. All the wooden framed windows and doors were fully opened, so we hurriedly closed them to contain some of the heat, because it was a bitterly cold day. They then made their beds and lay on them, because no chairs were available for relaxing in any of the billets. They started chatting about the service, and some officers in particular, especially one officer who worked in a certain office, who, because of his position made life particularly difficult for a large number of very young respectable volunteers in recruits division. Another officer whom they referred to as Hock, was not thought of as being a bad officer, but he certainly took his responsibility as the officer in control of the training division very seriously indeed. I shall refer to him in detail at a later stage. Then at 12.30, the Boatswain's whistle started again over the loudhailer, this time a long string of meaningless noises for about two minutes. I again asked the others what the hell was going on. "Oh", they answered casually, "that's the pipe for dinner!" "Isn't it very early for that?" I asked. "I'm only after having a feed of depth charges, and I'm sure they haven't even started to digest yet".

Anyway, I followed the others down, and just like breakfast time, the place was packed with young fellows and the noise of everyone shouting was deafening. But once inside you quickly got accustomed to it, since you are shouting just like the remainder of them. I couldn't exactly make out what they were eating, because most of them had both arms around the food and their heads down over it, as if someone was about to steal it. They were definitely drinking soup, and the dinner looked like roast beef and turnips, but I couldn't be sure until I collected my own at the wooden hatch. I passed "Ingo" again on the way in and he was covered in a smelly oily stink, and drenched with water after spilling the contents of a bucket over himself. The "Chef" at the hatch recognised me at once and referred to me as a "Townie". "What's your name and where are you from?" I said. "Ballyer", he said. "But how did you know I was after joining up?" He replied that someone had told him a neighbour of his arrived down the night before and he promised them that since I was from his area, he would look after me. He said his name was Larry O'Toole, and that there was a mistake with the cooking of the dinner. "What was the mistake, Larry?" I asked. "Well, I put the corned beef into the oven instead of boiling it, and it's ruined. It tastes alright, and it looks ok, and none of the others have noticed anything wrong. When you go back to the table, don't say a word, and I'll give you an extra spoon of potato, and a cup of tea in here in the cookhouse later on, when all the others have left". Remembering what I heard earlier about his gang adding browning to the tea, to give it some colour and body, I declined his generous offer.

I returned to our table and as promised I didn't reveal Larry's little secret. A little later, Ingo announced to all that were present that second helpings of spuds and "roast beef" were on offer, because some of the others on rations were gone ashore, and wouldn't be calling for dinner. A few who certainly looked hungry and half dead gratefully accepted the invitation. I never found out if they suffered the consequences. Since it was Saturday, there was a fairly decent dessert available. It was jelly and custard and I managed three helpings, Paddy O'Reilly's, Tony Keating's and my own. We then finished up and again returned to the billet, because there was simply nowhere else to go, and the weather was too cold to remain outdoors.

Inside another recruit like myself, "Barney", introduced me to another very useful and resourceful individual, a young fellow of medium height called "Wong". During my period down in Haulbowline, he made life for me and the others just that bit more bearable. He was let's say good with his hands, and when I was introduced to him, he was finishing embroidering work on one of the badges on his uniform jacket. "Wong" politely asked me did I want embroidery done or a cap ribbon or flashes sewn onto my no 1 uniform. I said I didn't, explaining that I wasn't being issued with a kit until Monday morning. "Well then" he said, "what do you want, a pass signed?" Brendan McGrane then roared across from the far side of the partition, "show him the officers' book then". "Wong" went to his wooden kit box and removed a neat sheet of paper from an envelope and written on the paper were the name of all the junior officers in the naval base who were obliged to perform the unpleasant task of duty officer in turn. Beside the name of each officer, he had written his own hand-written version of each officer's signature, which he had copied from discarded forms retrieved from bins around the establishment. In those days if you were going ashore during working hours, staying overnight ashore, or fancied a weekend away with your family or girlfriend (if you were that lucky) you needed a pass signed by the officer of the day, or your divisional officer. So, if he refused it, usually on the advice of the NCO and if everything looked hopeless, you simply approached "Wong" when he was in a good mood, and he asked which officer was on duty, or who was your divisional officer. "Hock" and "Firebox", were dead easy, because they were just long scribbles. Blundells, Yank O'Mahony, "Snags" Sutton, "Chase Me" William Anthony Murray or "Wam", were difficulty because they signed theirs clearly, but "Wong" was a professional, and none of us were ever caught, and none of the officers ever found out that their signatures were forged in the name of fair play for the rank and file. Wong should have received a medal for services rendered far beyond the call of duty.

Later I was standing chatting to a large group in the billet and in marched a rough looking Dublin gurrier, named "Muxer, also from Ballyer, and immediately he spotted me he asked, where in fucking hell did I get the clobber that I was wearing. I replied "in Burtons, in Dame Street, Dublin". "When, in 1920?" he said. All present laughed except the culchies and one of them, Paddy Burke, from West Cork, asked "What's a clobber?" Muxer shouted, with a wide grin on his small round face "a suit, you mulchy", don't youse bogmen understand plain English?"

A number of them then returned to cleaning their kits again. This endless cleaning and tidying is extremely boring to watch. First, the black winter cap is taken out and brushed. Then the white summer one is stripped of its bobbin and its brass badge at the front ,and then the ribbon with Éire embroidered on it is removed. A block of whitening is then produced and a toothbrush is used to whiten the cap, the canvas belt and the leggings. When this is completed, everything is hung up to dry. When the white cap and belt are dry, the brass badge and belt buckles are shined with Brasso until they glitter. Next to be cared for is the white front, a light cotton sleeveless garment with an Irish harp embroidered into it. This is washed and ironed with great care and attention. Then the two piece blue wool uniform is taken out of the kit box. It is carefully brushed with a clothes brush to remove the grey fluff that continuously falls from the blankets covering the beds. Both parts of the uniform are then turned inside out and pressed to ensure that the creases in the jacket and trousers are facing in. That is the regulation naval style. Next the lanyard similar to a small white rope is washed very carefully, along with the blue silk scarf and the very attractive blue jean collar with the anchors situated on each corner. That vital piece of dress wear is also lovingly ironed to reveal the creases facing outwards. Most importantly of all are the boots and shoes, it's spit and polish for hours on end. In recruits a group that is put together is referred to as a class, and if any member of that class decides in his own mind to start working on his kit, the others watching will automatically follow because the next day on the parade ground, nobody in that collection will ever allow himself to be shown up by the NCO in charge, since he will receive a bollocking from him, and his comrades will also make fun of him afterwards ashore, at meal time, in the billets, or wherever they may be. Therefore, that vicious circle creates a strong team and each recruit class are justly proud of that bond and dare anyone attempt to break it.

I watched this cleaning drill for about two hours, when, suddenly the duty PO, "Camel Driver" O'Keeffe marched in, (a nickname acquired from prolonged boasting to his cronies in the NCO's mess about his supposed heroic escapades with Monty at El-Alamein during World War Two. However, he ordered me to follow him up to the bedding stores. I mentioned to him that it was about time that I was issued with a new bed, because the one allocated to me last night is only fit for a pig". "You're not getting a new bed Brady", he angrily replied, "only a pillow slip, two sheets and another blanket. So shut up, your bed is just the same as the others". And me dreaming that I would have my own room with some carpet. He brought me up a hill near the jail, through a small gate, and along a garden and into a converted house with a sign over the door stating "Bedding Stores". Inside, the place was packed to the ceiling with mattresses, sheets, pillow slips, and hard pillows. He handed me the two sheets and pillow slip, that I was entitled to, and produced a large thick ledger book with FF again stamped on the cover. Here he said, "sign for that lot". I copied the style of the others in the book, and wrote Brady, James.

I walked back and joined the others, and as luck would have it, a couple of them were making up their beds. So this time I followed each of their movements with the greatest of concentration, because I was determined at the first attempt to get this right. When I opened up the sheets to use them, I discovered with horror that they were damp after lying up in that semi-derelict building they called the "Bedding Stores". So I opened them fully and placed them around the large steel radiators that were heating the buildings. Immediately after I placed them on the heat, the dampness started to dry out and it formed a light coloured cloud. Two hours later I removed them and the pillow slip and made up my bed similar to the others in the room. I looked proudly at my work and I was very happy because now, I said to myself, I have a bed to myself for the first time in my life!

At the sound of the whistle which by now I was

beginning to acknowledge, a large group of us rambled down for tea. Everywhere was extremely quiet due to the fact that it was the weekend, and a large percentage of the servicemen, especially the married ones, were gone ashore, mostly to Cobh. There was also very few in the dining hall, and only the duty cook, Peter Matthews looking sparkling in his spotlessly clean cooking jacket and chef's hat was there, with the inevitable "Ingo" again washing and storing thousands of dishes and mountains of cutlery. Peter announced very calmly that there was very little choice on the menu. "Your choice", he told every diner, "is to take it or leave it, because the food stores forgot to leave out your supplies". "What's the choice?" Georgie Long shouted. "Well George" he said, "all I can offer is scrambled eggs for ye all, and a couple of slices of toast thrown in, and I'll make a good strong cup of tea that you could trot a mouse on". I foolishly questioned the use of browning to Matthews and was immediately subjected to a tirade of unprintable abuse, the likes of which I had never before or since encountered. After a while he produced several thick slices of hard white bread burned rather than toasted, but he wasn't the worst of them (worse were to follow).

That night it was decided that a gang of them would hit the town of Cobh since it was Saturday, and the women were bound to be out in large numbers just hoping to meet them. "Stretch", "Doyler", "Muxer", "Hector", "The Blusher", "Maxie McCullagh", "Cider" and Hano, plus another group of ABs descended on the washhouse, and while some again attempted to shave they only again succeeded in nicking themselves with their razors. The others as natural as could be stripped naked in front of one another and then they started to sing completely out of tune Elvis Presley's current hit. They spent the best part of two hours cleaning every part of their bodies, and finishing with the old spice aftershave. Some of them even put talcum powder into their shoes, and Georgie Long produced the Brylcreem for his black curly hair. They were wondering why I wasn't joining them, but I lied and said I hadn't enough money. Redmond said he could lend me five bob, but I said "no, you'll need it yourself especially if you shift a bird". My real reason for not going out was because of the heap of rags I was dressed in. The others were wearing new suits they had bought in Cork, and by hook or by crook I was determined to acquire one as soon as humanly possible.

They all rushed down to catch the ten past seven boat to Cobh, but they were politely told by the duty PO that all launches in or out of the island were cancelled due to the bad weather and the high wind, by order of the duty CO. When they returned to the billet, I could see from their faces that they were bitterly disappointed, but not for long for they then decided to make their own enjoyment up in the wet canteen. The ratings canteen is simply another flat roofed limestone building left over from the British, and it's divided in two. The left side has a grocery shop fitted to cater for the needs of the housewives living in the married quarters, and stocks the requirements of the sailors for the proper upkeep of their uniforms. Also operated on that section is the tea room, that helped save the lads from starving to death. To the right as you enter is the wet, or the alehouse, where they never ask your age, address, or even your preferred sex. Like every military bar, the drink is cheaper there than anywhere else, simply because it's almost non-profit making, and it has no overheads like insurance, heating, lighting, staff, or indeed decorating. The Department of Defence pays for that lot. A pint of Guinness in those days was about one shilling and two pence (around six new pence), and we could easily get drunk on five bob (25p in today's money).

However, "Cider" ordered the usual, a flagon of Bulmers, McCullagh, Long, Doyler, Hano, Hector, and the Blusher called for pints of Guinness, and then Stretch asked what I wanted. I had never before touched alcohol, but I had heard the name Carlsberg some place, so I confidently said "I only drink bottles of Carlsberg lager. Three quarters of an hour later, we were joined by two beautiful young ladies from the married quarters. Newly wed Breda Fahy was slim and blond with a marvellous body and was the undoubted forces sweetheart for many years. Rory McCarthy's wife was her partner, another gorgeous woman from Dublin with a couple of kids. Both their husbands were on duty. So on that stormy night unable to leave Haulbowline, this was the only entertainment available. We of course bought them a few rounds of drink, and after a while a sing song started. Since Breda is from Cork, she tried a very boring version of *On the Banks of My Own Lovely Lee*. Hano attempted *The Holy Ground*, but he too was completely out of tune. After a while Doyler returned to the billet and to our surprise produced an accordion, and began to play professionally, tune after tune to everybody's delight. Simple and basic entertainment, yes, but if you are living on an island and marooned therein, you provide your own, and make do with what you've got. However, at ten o'clock closing time, the manager, known as the "Swamper" threw us out, and Tit Murtagh, half drunk, asked Breda could he leave her home. "It's alright", she replied, "I only live across the road". "Well, it's no harm trying!" The others carried cider back. I was unable to help because I was swaying from side to side after finishing four bottles of lager.

That night, I went straight into my own bunk and fell fast asleep until "The Camel Driver" woke me at 7am and reminded everyone present to make sure to be on church parade in their No 1 uniform. Everyone of them quickly hopped out of their beds. Some were wearing underpants, others had only the bottom parts of their pyjamas on, and a few, including Stretch Lynch were in their birthday suits. In fact Stretch always slept that way. He quietly said to me that everything gets well ventilated that way, and I readily agreed that he did have a good point. Then back into the washhouse where the high spirits and general messing continued as usual. Another new recruit was physically stripped and scrubbed under a very warm shower because the occupants of another billet said he was filthy, and that he never cleaned himself, which goes to prove that if you are a member of a pack, you must conform or be forced to do so. After everyone had finally finished attempting again to shave a soft smooth face covered in pimples, we made our way back to the dining hall. Everything was of course as usual. Peter Matthews was still on duty and really trying his best with what was available. He did, however, manage to make the fried eggs look like burned pancakes, but at least he was trying and he was willing. I was satisfied that eventually he would make a terrific chef and that we would all be extremely proud of him.

For once Ingo was missing, so the Duty PO then ordered George Carr, who very reluctantly and finally, under the threat of the CO or the Guard Room, took in hand the unhappy task of washing several hundred dishes and cutlery, plus cleaning out the dining room, and the cookhouse, and helping with the peeling of several sacks of potatoes before dinner. So back again to the billet and the boredom is just beginning to set in. It's this daily routine with no diversions and so little to do. The entire group in the room then set about changing into their No 1s, and to get into the top of the uniform, you needed the help of another, because it was not possible to undertake that task yourself, since the jacket was made almost skintight, and because it was so tight, you required a friend to pull it down over your head. While removing it, you again required the same attention. Today, that operation is much simpler because all the jackets are fitted with buttons and open just like any gent's coat.

At precisely 8am, another untrained high-pitched country lad's voice over the loudhailer shouted "All hands to church parade" and then when all were accounted for, they were inspected by the duty officer and marched down to the naval church. I looked from one of the windows above, and observed the first ever group of naval personnel on parade, and I was somewhat impressed at their clean and smart appearance, and of course, their confident footwork and instant response to the NCO's command. His first order sounded like "Ryan Eirre", and then they all snapped their boots together to attention. His next roar was like "Goo Rare Clay, Goo Maher Ma Shawl", and then they all marched off through the arch and the two sides of the main wooden gates were automatically

The author shortly before enlisting, outside our house in Ballyfermot. My mother bought that rigout for twelve and sixpence, about 62p.

The advert that lured me into the service.

Jailers outside the guardroom, their commander is on the left. The Haulbowline crest is over the door.

Ferriter, left, instructing my recruits class on the square. Stretch is third from the left.

Recruits under instruction. Early 1950's some of the precision equipment.

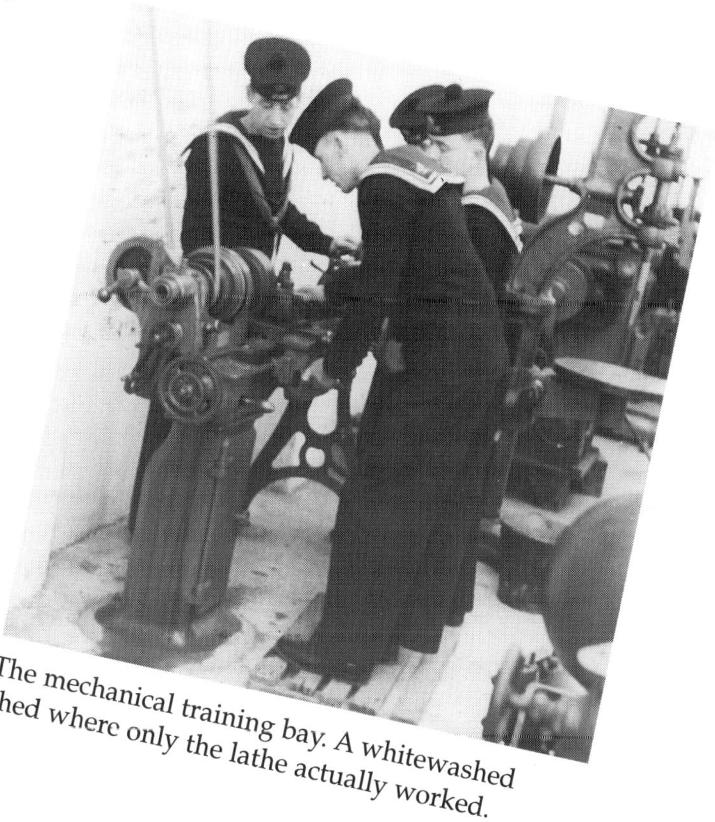

The mechanical training bay. A whitewashed shed where only the lathe actually worked.

Christmas Party aboard Maev in 1957. Author extreme left; Stretch centre; Hector on his left.

Hector, Roche, Stretch, and Fleming aboard Macha. Note horrible army overalls on Roche and Stretch.

The forward boiler-room on board Maev. It was hell!

Cook Dunworth in a sparkling white uniform posing for the camera while serving us the bacon and cabbage on the Cliona.

Seán Lemass inspecting a guard of honour at Irish Steel in 1954.

Macha, second from right alongside Brest, France in 1951.

L.E. Macha, ex-H.M.S. Borage entering Cork Harbour. The deck crew is facing Cobh.

L.E. Maev, ex-H.M.S. Oxlip.

L.E. Cliona ex-H.M.S. Belworth at anchor in Cork harbour shortly after arrival from Britain, complete with a wooden mast.

"Mugu" with cane explaining part of a depth charge to a class of new recruits.

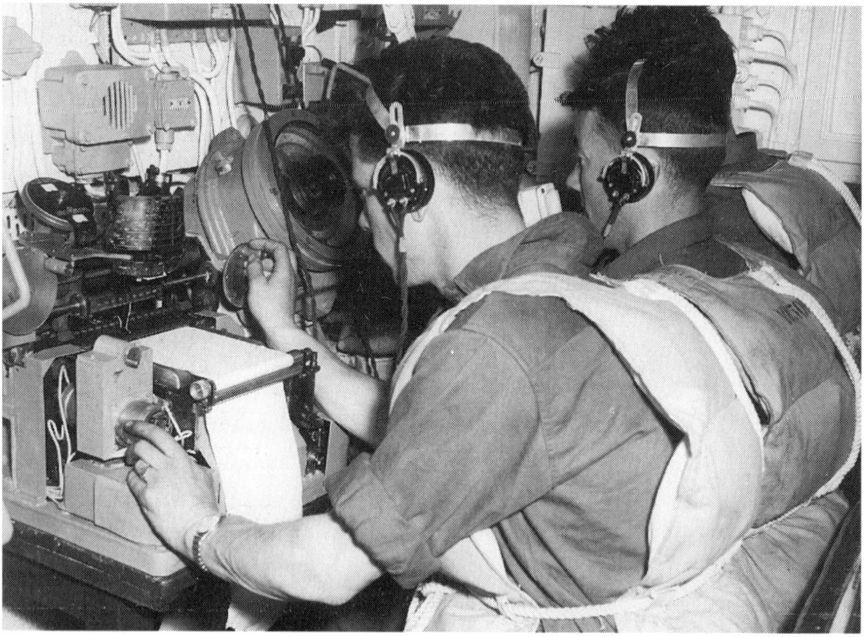

Asdic crew at action stations aboard the Macha in the 1960's.

opened to allow them an uninterrupted journey to catch the ten past eight mass.

I was the only one remaining, and the place seemed very quiet and almost eerie after the others had left. So I decided that since I had nothing better to do, and since I hadn't attended mass, I would join my colleagues. I managed to catch up with the parade just as they entered the Church of Our Lady Star of the Sea. I was surprised at how basic it actually was. The church was adorned by a large mural of Our Lady, and along the walls of each side were several paintings depicting sailors at sea in inadequate boats, and so I naturally wondered to myself what sort of condition are our ships really in. Then I noticed how segregated this house of God was, and how it is practised even during worship. The top left hand side was occupied by the Commanding Officer and his wife, then to his right was the second in command and his wife, then his juniors. Behind that group were the Senior NCOs, and next the junior NCOs. Sitting close to the door were the recruits and then the civilians living on the island. As the mass progressed, the church organ began to play beautiful soft music perfectly in tune, and then the church choir commenced singing in prefect harmony. They sang out, without the aid of any form of amplification, to the delight of everyone present, including of course, the naval chaplain. One member of that choir was Rory McCarthy, a father figure to all who required a guiding hand. During the performing of this great music and song, I looked around and spotted another CPO of average height with black wavy hair and a broad and strong looking body. In front of him were stacked a pile of Ireland's Own magazines, and he was deeply engrossed in one of them and actually laughing while the mass was in progress. When the service was concluded he insisted that I purchase one from him, and on my return journey back to the billet, I asked Mick Buckley who that extraordinary CPO was. All he said was, "that's the famous 'Batt' Sullivan and you'll be hearing and seeing plenty of him". Boy was he right (that was the under-statement of the year).

After another forgettable lunch and with nothing better to do, I asked the others who the CO was, the man with the three gold stripes on his sleeves, who was sitting up at the top of the church where everybody could admire him. "That's Tommy McKenna and he lives up there in the biggest house behind the flagpole on the square, and from up there, he can see everything that's going on all around him. When he sees anything happening out of the ordinary, he simply rings the guardroom looking for the duty PO or duty officer to go down and take care of things, and if anybody is put on a charge, they are brought up before him for punishment". The barrack room lawyer, "Barney" then interrupted and volunteered the information that Tommy was in fact the prosecutor, the judge and the jury. "I see" I said. I was still learning the ropes, but very rapidly now. "Well what about his right hand man?" "Well" Johnny Hart said, "that's Petie Kavanagh Lt-Cmdr. Someone told me he had a few ships sunk from under him during the war. Doyler said, "Wasn't that rather unfortunate?" "How do you mean unfortunate, because the ships were sunk or because Petie was saved?" So they went on and on until they again turned their full attention to the main topic of conversation, the girls! Much later, I did a little checking on both their backgrounds, and an in-depth investigation into the gentleman who was directing this outfit, a certain former Royal Navy Officer, Commander HJAS Jerome, DSO, or Jake, as we referred to him. I will explain my findings later on.

After forcing down a tea consisting of potato cakes made from left overs from dinner, and home made currant cake which was as usual burned to a crisp, we all descended on the drill shed to support the base basketball team against a tired and untrained squad from one of the ships. Jack Banim from the base group suffered a severe cut to his face after being pushed to the floor of the shed by an eighteen stone farmer's son from Kilkenny. But despite his severe bleeding from his wound, he refused to attend the "Hospital" because he was aware that the Doc, was on duty. He chose instead to patch up his wound until he could find a civilian doctor ashore that night and pay for his services out of his own pocket, or wait until an army doctor visited the island the following morning on his regular call. The name "Doc" should be self explanatory for Jack's refusal to attend for treatment.

A Full Kit

Later that evening the culchies in the billet went ashore to Cobh to attend a Ceilí and while doing his rounds Sam Bass O'Hara casually remarked that Cocoa and bread and jam was on the menu in the cookhouse for supper at 7.30pm for recruits only. Nobody paid any attention to him and to my knowledge, that subject was never mentioned again. Since the others were all gone out, I decided to retire to the bunk early, but I was rudely interrupted by the bogmen who were practising Irish dancing around the solid wooden floor in their issued hob-nailed boots. However, I dragged myself out of the sack at 7 o'clock, with the remainder of them and again borrowed a towel and soap from Stretch, and when we returned to prepare for COs parade at 9 o'clock, Sam Bass O'Hara ordered me to the supply stores to collect my full kit. This crumbling building is situated on the East End of the parade ground and it is entered by two very heavy and reinforced wooden doors. To the left, as you enter was the secure gun compound, and in charge of that section was a great character, the armoured, an army Sergeant named Joey Cummins. To the right is the food store and to this day, I can still recall the beautiful smell of fresh bread, spices, puddings and above all, Tony Fahy, Breda's smart husband frying bacon, eggs, and sausages with a few onions thrown in to devour during their break. The aroma alone almost made me keel over for I was still starving after forcing down my breakfast only an hour earlier. To reach the clothing stores you then climbed a very wide open staircase, and on the large landing above, sailors' complete uniforms including boots and shoes, with very little wear were stored in hundreds of sacks reaching a height of approximately ten feet.

When I entered the heavily fortified room I asked the assistant the dour Johnny Wallace who would not use three words if one would do, if the uniforms outside were to be issued. His simple and straight forward answer was, no. Wallace then asked sourly what size hat I took and I replied that I never wore one. Then he asked what size shoes did I wear. I didn't know, because my mother always bought them for me. Then he asked what size coat did I wear. I didn't know that either, since my mother purchased them second hand, and there were never any size tags left on them. "Well, fuck you", he said very angrily. "Here then try that overcoat on. It might fit you, but you'll never be anything like its previous owner". The previous owner was a Warrant Officer during the emergency who had retired ten years earlier. He must have been an extremely tall man, because at that time, I was six foot one and a half and his coat almost reached my ankles. From a filthy and very dusty shelf, Wallace then proceeded to remove various parts of a naval uniform, and he then handed me a rough blue woollen trousers with a front which opens very easily. After a while, he surprisingly volunteered the information that the easy opening and the bell buttons were designed for simple disposing of in case of shipwreck. Again, I wondered was I going to sea in a sieve. I inquired as to where the fitting room was, and he answered without any expression on his face, "where you're standing!", and then he ordered "here, try those shoes on and that cap", and so forth until he declared himself satisfied that I was fully fitted out. Then he went outside to the landing, opened up a sack, emptied its contents of dirty and torn towels onto the floor, and said, "here's your clothing bag". I then signed for everything and left quickly for I couldn't wait to return to wash everything in our billet.

On the way down the stairs I happened to meet the officer in charge, a certain ensign called Johnny White who had only just been promoted from the ranks and I asked him why I was presented with so much army kit, which included army grey woollen socks, belt, leggings, boots, and worst of all, army working overalls, complete with brass buttons. This highly respected officer gently replied that the army authorities actually run the navy, and that we take what we receive from them, and furthermore, he said that our boss was only a captain, and so only equivalent to a Colonel in the army, and that they are two a penny. "Thank you Sir", I said. "Now I am beginning to understand the position". Then I asked about the pile of good uniforms that were heaped up on the landing. "Oh" he said, "they are for collection by a Jew man. They are being scrapped because they were left behind by deserters and troublemakers who were dishonourably discharged.

I then rushed across to the others to firstly empty everything out of the filthy clothing sack, wash what was possible, especially the white fronts with the blue ring around its sides and the harp on its front. I then visited the indispensable "Wong", and handed him two shillings to sew onto my cap a bobbin, a ribbon and pin the gold coloured cap badge into its proper position. When he had completed his professional handy work, he returned a very attractive cap which was ideal for my No 1 parade duties. I then handwashed everything in hot lux soap flakes which I had acquired from Hector to remove every musty smell from the stores, and that damn sack that Wallace called a clothing bag. Later on when everything was dry I borrowed the electric iron from next door, and over a period of about two and a half hours, I lovingly ironed every item of clothing naval style, under the watchful eyes of Doyler and Stretch. When everything was completely satisfactory, I then for the first time tried on my new navy suit, and from their guidance and instructions, and trial and error, I eventually learned how to wear my No 1s.

The Dreaded Drill NCO

Shortly after our tea break in the canteen, George Carr told me that Timmy Ferriter wanted to see me immediately in the drill shed, and when I arrived, he was standing to attention and completely erect with a rifle in his right hand. As I entered, he shouted, "Sonny, when you speak to me, make sure you are standing to attention, and address me as "Sir'!" "Yes, Sir!" I answered, in a frightened voice. He continued by saying that he was the Chief Petty Officer in charge of training, and by the time he was finished with me he would have either made me or broken me, and that before long, I would probably be running home to my mother crying. During all this bullshit talk, he was continuously sneezing and coughing straight into my face, and each time he sneezed, his saliva contaminated with tobacco burned my eyes and entered my mouth when I attempted to respond to his bollocking and bullying. Only afterwards, did I discover that he suffered from a severe form of catarrh. He finally finished by saying that a recruits' class was already in progress for two weeks, and since I was on my own, and not belonging to any class, he had decided that I would join the advanced class the following morning, and because of this, I had better smarten myself up if I wished to stay in the service. "Yes, Chief, Sir", I answered. "Now, go back up to that billet and try to learn something from the others".

That night, for hour after hour, the remainder of them were shouting orders from every side of the building. "Goo rare maker shawl! Aire! Umpig art! Goo moule maher shawl!", and then with the rifle "See hig arms! too hig arms lage-ig-arms!", all Irish names, I was told, and funnily enough, nobody present could tell the English versions of that lot, except "Attention!" Around the billet that night, I must have walked at least twenty miles in bloody brown army boots that I had forgotten to dye with a black colour I had purchased along with a block of whitening, with a loan of a few bob from another good recruit, Tom Kendrick. However, I eventually finished my dying and whitening of my leggings and belt and the colouring of the boots they called "chounders'. I completed everything after 1am, and went straight to bed completely exhausted, after my first day's training.

The next morning I was awake well before seven,

waiting for the call the hands roar. I felt like a well trained and well fed professional athletic at the starting line rearing to go and get it over with. So at 8.20 we were told to fall in line inside the drill shed to be inspected and drilled in private, before we were allowed on to the square beside the remainder of the base personnel, and of course, the CO, 2 IC, and the Navy Chaplain. "Brady!" CPO Ferriter roared. "If you fucking make a show of me or the rest of us out on that square, you'll be sorry you were ever born. I will run you around this fucking island ten times with a full kit until you drop". "Ye, ye, yes, yes, Chief, I won't let anyone down". "OK let's see some smart footwork, Sonny", he said. "Brady only. Shass eige a Rash". I responded by putting my right foot out and putting my hands behind my back. He shouted very angrily "have you got two fucking right feet?" followed by, "you broke your mother's heart, but you won't break mine and, "you have a face only a mother could love". Again, Brady, only. Shass eige a Rash, and put your left foot out if you have one". This time, I did it properly. "Now you, Brady, Goo rare clay, go maher, Ma Shawl". I started marching with my right foot forward instead of the left and then walked straight into the white-washed wall. "You, Brady, are not going on to that square to make a laugh of us". He then demanded that leading Seaman, Trooper O'Shea be detailed to teach me some footwork and manners. I spent two full days with the Trooper in the drillshed until I was allowed near that parade ground, after which the unfortunate Trooper, an ex-army man was mentally and physically exhausted. At least I now knew how to walk and to answer to orders, even though I didn't know what they meant in English.

Oddly enough, when I returned to our living quarters each evening after my gruelling ordeals, none of the others slagged me and believe me, I was thankful for that small mercy, because those fucking hob-nailed army boots were cutting the bloody feet off me. If I had the ready cash then, I would have gladly paid someone a good price to break them in for me. Over the next several days, I gradually learned by heart the various commands from the instructors on the square. I was now at least qualified to accompany the others onto the parade ground and as I marched alongside them or stood beside them, I fully concentrated with both eyes on their movements just to be positive that I got the drill correct. That was the first occasion that I made myself do something positive, and I could feel that I was maturing at a steady rate. We moved about the entire base as a class, a distinct unit who did everything as one. I quickly learned other commands in Irish, including "Go moule Ma Shawl! Heart Umpig! Clay Umpig! Das Umpig! Layge Amac! Layge Isteach!", and so forth. That's not the correct spelling, but that's how they sounded to me. So it continued over and over until we got everything right. During all this hardship, I often wondered what the hell has the parade ground got to do with sailing ships, and in my mind, I held the army responsible for this crazy situation, because they had and still have full control of the navy, and intensely disliked us.

Housed in a Haunted Billet

However, the officer in charge of the training division, Hock, decided to move us across the road to the upper arch billet, because our rooms were required for a potential NCOs course, which was about to commence. The arch buildings are so called, because to enter them, you must walk under an arch. Those billets are not fitted with central heating of any kind, the heat being generated by an ancient solid fuel burning stove situated at one end. That stove was later to prove very useful as a means of cooking food which was secured by us by very dodgy circumstances, but we were losing weight very rapidly from the miles of marching every day and food obtained by whatever means, helped to supplement our near starvation diet. Although we had now lost the excellent view of the mouth of the harbour, which we greatly enjoyed in the main billets, the upper arch was much cosier, the wooden windows didn't rattle during the gales, officers didn't frequent the place regularly, and it was much quieter since far less people in general walked through it.

But there was one major drawback to all those minor advantages that I have just mentioned. The shagging place was haunted, and still is, and nobody said a word. They simply allowed us to walk literally straight into a trap. Speedy Thornton and Brendan McGrane and others were quietly going about their boring duties, of washing, polishing and ironing, when all of a sudden, their tiny valve radio turned itself off. So they disconnected its three pin plug, checked the leads, the plug and the fuse, then plugged it back in and still it refused to work, despite the fact that the socket itself was live and all the lights worked in the room. So they therefore assumed that the radio was faulty and forgot about it. Then suddenly to their horror, it came back on again then off again then back on and it remained that way. Shortly after that they nearly died when they observed several British soldiers walking around the room in First World War uniforms with heavy boots and leggings. Some even had field dressings covering flesh wounds. This was all observed in broad daylight, and in normal working hours. So a number of them approached the chaplain and related the happenings to him, but strangely he dismissed them out of hand, replying that they must have been dreaming, or had a large amount of alcohol taken. When they reported this back to the others, the barrack room lawyer Barney, called a conference to discuss the case, and after a heated debate with several suggestions from all sides, it was finally agreed by a show of hands that they would appeal their case personally to the bishop living in Cobh for his directions. But the billets' NCO PO Cantwell heard of the scheme and warned them if they proceeded with their case, they would be on the next train home. So that ended that, or so we thought.

The following morning, McGrane and Barney quietly asked me was there anyone interfering with my bunk during the previous night. I answered not that I knew of, since I had not woken during the entire night. They reported to me that someone or something was pulling at the springs of their beds all through the night and that they were very frightened throughout the entire ordeal. I completely forgot about that conversation until the following Monday night / Tuesday morning, when I suddenly awoke for no apparent reason at exactly a quarter to three, because the base's clock was ringing out that time. The billet was absolutely quiet and nobody was snoring and nobody was walking around the place after being to the toilet, and most importantly, it was a very still night, with no wind blowing. So, therefore, I wondered for a few moments why I should have woken up and then I turned slightly to my left in order to return to sleep, when all of a sudden I felt a very strong pressure on my stomach pressing in and then out, rather like if you were breathing heavily after running a long distance. This pressure was not of a solid nature, just soft, but a strong weight, pressing downwards, and then releasing it. Immediately I remembered what the others had told me the previous week about their beds being interfered with. Then, I assumed that it was the spirit or spirits of British soldiers, and I then used some language that they would clearly have understood. I simply said "Will you now fuck off, and I will pray for you". Then I blessed myself and said the few promised prayers and returned to sleep without further interference.

The next day I reported my strange event to one of the oldest serving persons in the Navy, CPO "Paddles" McKeown (so called because he had very large feet). He said that it was believed that a British soldier had hung himself in the corner I was sleeping in. I reported that vital piece of news back to the others, and they watched my reactions for any signs of weakness. So, I decided not to move my bed from the area, simply because I would have had to endure terrible treatment from the remainder of them and they would have branded me a coward, and weaklings were not their kind of people. As I mentioned earlier, if you are in a pack, you go with the pack or else. Many years later, I spoke to a very well known medium, and I explained everything about my experience except what "Paddles" McKeown had told me. I was astounded when he replied that someone had hung himself over my bed and the pressure I felt on my stomach was similar to what he was suffering when he was cut down, because he was gasping for breath. This worry and tension, plus the fact that a few of them in the billet insisted on returning to the subject made life rather trying, especially since we were doing our best to grasp the foot drill and marching orders transmitted in the Irish language which was alien to all of us. But it certainly hardened us for what lay ahead: Rifle drill; the regulation approach to the proper upkeep of your weapon; range practice; the specialised training in your chosen branch of the service, and above all, an extremely difficult future aboard bitches of ships at sea in all weathers. That I shall also refer to later.

Rifle Drill & Good Pay

When we were in a reasonable straight line, and in step, "Hock" and Timmy Ferriter announced that we should now begin training in the use of the rifle. The next morning, after parade, we were all marched up to Sergeant Joey Cummins in the supply stores to draw out a Lee-Enfield, a sling to carry it, and a short bayonet to suit this new type gun that had only been delivered the year before. The numbers from each weapon were read out and entered in a large ledger, and beside the number you signed your name, making you responsible for its safe keeping. Therefore, no matter what happened to it, you were held responsible. If it went missing or God forbid it was stolen, all you could do was pray, because unaccounted for ammunition, displaced weapon parts, or lost guns were hanging offences, with no way out. All that was drilled into us everywhere we went. Food, clothing, machinery parts, and personnel could vanish, and could be easily replaced, but anything that originated in the armourer's store was sacred and was simply irreplaceable. So when we signed for that rifle, we continuously watched it, even when it was chained into the gun cabinet in our room. We checked and rechecked the weapons by their serial numbers each time we walked by just to make doubly sure it was safe and sound. Each bayonet was also secured by lock and key in our strong wooden kit boxes, although some of the more adventurous red arses, with plenty of energy and nothing better to do, frequently used them as daggers, and sometimes as drills to bore large holes in the wooden floors. A few were real professionals, who without aiming, always managed to hit a market target from a long distance. Looking back now it was of course a very dangerous practice since others were sleeping close by. Anyway, rifle drill thankfully wasn't commencing until Monday morning, and pay day was tomorrow, Friday, at 12 noon in the drill shed.

Since I started down there, the subject of rates of pay was quite simply never brought up, maybe because we were preoccupied with just holding ourselves together, so that we would not crack up under the strain of living in this strange and weird environment. Everybody was naturally flat broke, and my ten shillings was well spend on cakes, biscuits and mugs of tea up in the canteen. So eventually we made our way into the drillshed at ten to twelve under the illusion that if we arrived early, we would be paid early and then we could immediately proceed straight up to the canteen for another good feed before our dinner of boiled white fish, peas and potatoes, oh and potato and pea soup. When we entered the place it was full to near overflowing and believe it or not, this gathering was also segregated. Senior NCOs were grouped together, and so were the junior NCOs. Next in line were the ABs. Then came the newly trained personnel and last in line to be paid were the unfortunate red arse recruits. So, thinking of it, I reckoned that we would be lucky to get out of the place by 1.30, just before parade time again. So when an AB was paid, I begged a loan of five bob from him and then went to the canteen for a life-saving meal. When I returned, they were ready to call us, and then we marched up towards the pay officer and his assistant, Paddy Smith. Everyone was served in alphabetical order. Therefore Aherne was called first, then Barry, and then myself. Now I couldn't hear what amount they received, so when I reached the counter, I didn't know what to expect, then Paddy Smith said to the officer, "Brady, James, Sir, two pounds and nine pence". I assumed he meant for a day, so I said to the officer, "I'm in a week, Sir", and then perhaps not knowing exactly what I had said, he replied "no talking during pay parade". Jack Brennan, who heard me correctly remarked to me "You should go ashore, meet a girl, get married, have a few kids, and then you would be entitled to mickey money. I picked up the few shillings and walked back to consult with the others, including the barrack Lawyer, "Barney", in a state of near mortal shock. Barney was as usual, reassuring. Lying on his bed smoking a Golden Virginia, "roll your own cigarette", he simply said, "look at it this way. Here you are on a beautiful island, surrounded by a lovely sea, with plenty of fresh air, and away from those smelly buses and cars up in Dublin. The food here is not exactly up to the Gresham Hotel standards, neither is the accommodation. But you receive a free kit and a lovely uniform that you could wear anywhere, and the instructors on the square take care of you just like your mother did". I was just then on the verge of crying when someone picked up one of his heavy army boots, and threw it across the room which struck "Barney" on the back of the head, which almost knocked him out, at least it shut him up.

With so little cash I was in deep trouble. I was expecting to send the mother around a fiver a week to help feed the other eight hungry kids left with her. I was also hoping to somehow replace the rags that I had arrived in, for I was fed up with the laughing I was getting while I was wearing them. I had also hoped to go up to Cork this weekend and replace the lot with a complete new wardrobe, including shoes, socks, a tie, and nice underwear, but now I'm really in the shit. What the hell am I to do? There was only one option left open. I decided there and then to start saving hard immediately. Don't cut out the life saving food like the depth charges, just the frills, like cakes, biscuits, sweets and minerals, and in a matter of months, I should have sufficient funds and be in a strong position to move with confidence. I was determined that the new gear would be in my locker as soon as humanly possible, and that the women would follow soon after that because once they see the good quality clothes, they will assume that the money is also there. Yes, but what's to happen between now and then, because I've nothing left to wear except the uniform? From what I'd seen, very few went ashore to Cobh in the uniform. Therefore, I was well and truly up the creek. But then, the ever reliable Stretch helped me out again with the loan of a sports jacket and dark grey trousers and since he was only about an inch taller than myself, they were almost the right fit. I could use the navy's light blue No 1 boots, which weren't bad, once they were covered up with the trousers, and I could also used their blue stocking to match. Hector loaned me a light grey tie, Bobby Hume a shirt, and Tony Keating a maroon woollen neck jumper. Everything felt alright on me, so then I went out to the washhouse and examined the outfit from every angle in the mirrors. The Salmon poacher caught me admiring the outfit and said "hey, have you a big date ashore or are you going to a whorehouse in Cork? That's some style!" he added. "pity about the colour scheme!" I didn't answer because frankly, it looked ok to me. I then changed back into my drill gear, and hung everything up on a wire hanger, and stored it away in the locker until the following afternoon. That Friday afternoon we marched and drilled a little more and because Ferriter had an appointment ashore somewhere, we managed to finish a little earlier, and then after a horrible tea of scrambled eggs on toast, we sat around the billet listening to the radio for the entire evening, and again pressing clothes and brushing our uniforms and polishing our footwear until we could see our faces in them.

CO's Rounds

The next day was COs rounds, and the place must be handed over to him spotless with everything in place, and all the bedding on every bed matching each other and in perfect line. All footwear belonging to each recruit must also be in place at the foot of every bed, again matching one another. The floor was washed, then the lead swinger was brought into play, with poor Georgie Long unable to manage its heavy weight, until Brendan Halligan, as strong as an ox, was drafted in for the swinging of it. "Brady", said PO Cantwell, "You clean out the toilets, and I want them fucking spotless, and no fucking about". "Where's the gloves, PO?". I asked. "Hands were invented before gloves, and we don't use them down here, so get fucking on with it". "But PO, they are stinking!" "Do the fucking thing!" he shouted. "Yes, PO", I replied timidly.

The jacks were indeed foul after a gang of them including Cider O'Reilly, Doyler and Pints McEvoy had been down in the wet canteen until closing time the night before. Whatever they were drinking was like tar, because it was black and stuck to the bowl, and the smell was just unbelievable, and may I add, masks were unheard of in those days. So I searched around and found a bag of caustic soda and placed it around the bowls and left it as long as I could before flushing, and it worked wonders on three of them. But the fourth was completely stuffed as hard as hell, and I thought to myself, they must have been shitting bricks as well as drinking tar, which thinking back could have been that browning they were adding to the tea down in the cookhouse. Anyway, I was forced to place my hand and arm right down to the shoulder into the toilet bowl and remove a mixture of God knows what with a smell of something not belonging to this planet. That aroma stuck in my nose and head for many hours afterwards. Anyway, the undiluted jeyes fluid finally killed the smell, and I stood around making sure nobody touched those toilets or flushed away that life-saving jeyes fluid. "Alright", shouted Cantwell, "get back into the billet if you're finished there, and start shining the door handles and window latches with brasso". "Yes, PO". "And hurry up, he's due in ten minutes".

When the CO, Tommy McKenna arrived Cantwell demanded that I stand beside him during the inspection, and when McKenna entered the room Cantwell saluted and said "Sir, Upper Arch ready for your inspection". "Very well, PO", answered McKenna. "And who have we here?" asked McKenna, pretending to be interested in the rank and file. "Brady, Sir, he's only in a week, and learning fast". "Are you happy here, Brady?" "Yes, he is Sir", Cantwell answered quickly. "You are tall and fit looking", said McKenna. "Yes, Sir", I quickly replied before Cantwell could speak, "it's all the square bashing". "Well, it's good for you, Brady. Helps to make a man out of you, and in a few years, you could be a leading seaman". The future could be bright indeed. He then proceeded down to the lower arch, and then back to his office followed by the 2IC and Warrant Officer, Nick Kennedy. On my way down to join up, here was I thinking I could be an officer fairly soon. Ah well, where there's life there's hope, and anything could happen. We shall have to wait and see. The others drifted back after stuffing themselves in the civvy canteen outside the main gate. But Stretch as reliable as ever, with always a thought, brought me back two depth charges and a bottle of milk "on the house", he said, as he handed them over to me.

My First Love

After dinner Stretch and myself hurriedly dressed to catch the ten past two launch ashore in order to thoroughly examine Cobh in broad daylight. We caught the Department of Defence coal burning boat, the Sir John Wyndham, as she was ready to move away from the pier. She was almost full to her capacity of 120 passengers, which obviously included the naval people and their wives from the island, plus the soldiers and their families from Spike Island, going ashore to collect their weekend shopping. We reached our destination in approximately fifteen minutes, walked up the steps, then turned left towards the train station and the first two young ones whom we met, we said hello to, but they completely ignored us. I said to

Stretch, "Never mind, they could be deaf and dumb". So we simply walked on to the deep water quay and he said hi to a group of lovely girls who were talking to a crew member of the famous tug, the Turmoil. Again, the ladies completely ignored us, except for one standing behind, who responded to us by saying "Ye Dublin fuckers are in the Navy, and one of ye made my sister pregnant, and ye should go and fuck off and my mother warned me not to have anything to do with the likes of ye". I replied that we never even met her sister, that that this was our first time ashore. "And anyway, we didn't want anything off youse. All we said was hi". "It's not 'youse', you Dublin fucker", she said, "it's ye". "Things are looking bad", I said to Stretch. It could have been the clobbers we're dressed in and the colour schemes. Anyway, we then decided to ramble back up towards the heart of the town.

We passed the oldest yacht club in the world on our right, then the Garda Station directly opposite the naval pier and Stretch said "they are always watching the navy lads", "Why?" I said, "do they fancy some of them?" Then we walked along the people's park and opposite is the famous Commodore Hotel, then owned by a German gentleman who only opened it during the summer months and entry was excluded to naval personnel below officer rank, because the CO played cards there with his posy civvy friends. Another case I predicted for Barney the lawyer, to debate in the billets. Then down past the post office, and directly across was the then unfinished memorial dedicated to the Lusitania disaster which claimed over one thousand two hundred lives in 1915, many of whom are buried in mass graves in the old churchyard in Cobh. Down we went along West Beach, and East Hill, then straight down to the pilot's station, and then we decided to visit the majestic St Colman's Cathedral situated far above the town on a beautiful site overlooking the wide and glorious naturally made harbour. We entered this granite house of God and were completely overawed by the great care and dedication of hundreds of very skilled craftsmen over many years to produce such an unbelievable achievement, the likes of which I had simply never dreamed of seeing. After about two hours sitting in this magnificent building and studying the workmanship therein, we decided to study the remainder of the town. As we toured around, taking in as much as we could before darkness fell, we were struck by the large numbers of public houses available almost on every corner, and by the fact that there were no places to eat, or even have a cup of tea, and oddly enough, there were no Italian chippers. Much later, we did learn about the Soldiers' and Sailors' Rest, which provided food and shelter for those in need, and this service was ably managed by a Protestant lady, a Miss Batson, and a man we referred to as Lofty, as restaurant assistants. We and lots of others should be eternally grateful to them, because on many occasions, they provided accommodation to youngsters who were caught out in Cobh, after missing the last boat back to the base at ten past twelve at night, with the entire town in complete darkness and nowhere else to go, except perhaps if a train was in the station where they could sleep in an extremely cold carriage.

As we toured around, I recognised the Well House bar where I had encountered the sailor on the first night of my arrival, So I suggested to Stretch that we go inside and inspect the place. The interior was very drab and old fashioned, and the place badly required painting and decorating. The bar extended to the full length of the room, with seating to the right and left as you enter. The proprietor, who was also the only barman, looked about 45 years of age, and all I can remember about him was that he looked a little mad and certainly acted that way. As the pair of us approached the bar for service, he looked at us as if he had just seen a ghost, and then with a distinctly unfriendly voice, asked what we wanted. Stretch said "I'll have the usual, a Britvic orange". "And you?" "A bottle of Carlsberg, that's my usual". I handed him a pound note, which I had decided very reluctantly to break on, and then he handed me back nineteen shillings change and I knew that two drinks didn't only cost a shilling, even over in our wet canteen. I said nothing, and then we looked around for somewhere to sit with a good river view and in a position to watch out for the local talent that might walk by the window, or step inside looking for company, hopefully our company.

After a while I recognised the voices of Hano and Cider, who were excited over a game of darts, and to their left, Willie Mynes and Dermo Kelly were enjoying a harmless game of rings. I asked Hano about the weird looking man behind the bar who insisted on handing me the wrong change. "Ah", said Hano, "don't mind that gobshite, he's only after getting out of the madhouse, and he's in and out of there all the time". Then Cider added "it was the drink and the women. He could have handled one or the other, but not the two combined". "And what about the wrong change?" "Well, why do you think all the navy fellas drink here every night? He's keeping us going, sure we all bring in the birds and fall out of the place every night for half nothing. Because of his mental condition, he can't even remember the prices". Hano added "he's still living in the 1930s". "Right", I said to Stretch, "go up and call for two bottles of Carlsberg and forty Players Medium Cut, and four packets of Tayto crisp which have small packets of salt in them". I got the lot for three bob.

Around seven, two young girls walked in as if they owned the place, and they looked to me as cool as ice. They both walked up to the counter and said "Andy, may we have a glass of ale and an orange with plenty of ice please?" I was right they were cool, and by their accents they sounded like poshies. So since they sat at the table next to ours, I politely asked them were they from Dalkey. "No" the redhead replied, "we are from Cobh originally, but we have been abroad in England for some years. "And what part of Cobh are you from?" "Just up the hill, a place called Belmont". "Oh, I see, said Stretch. "What about yourself?" she asked, while looking very seriously at my clothes. "Are you an actor, or what?" "Well, yes, I've been acting in the Abbey since I was nine, and suddenly last week I got an unexpected call to the naval service after a performance, and would you believe, those bloody fools in CIE lost all my clothes in the luggage compartment on the way down". "That was hard luck", the redhead answered. "But I'm not worried, because I have demanded full compensation for everything". "And what about you?" the lovely little brunette asked Stretch. "Oh, I'm also from Dublin, and I'm with him". Then I handed him four bob and told him to buy a round for the four of us, and four more bags of crisps and peanuts. My two quid wages was rapidly disappearing, but I didn't care because this was my first encounter with the opposite sex, and with every sip of Carlsberg, that redhead was growing more beautiful. Stretch was chatting to the other one about the North Strand, the Howth Road, and his area of East Wall and the Liffey Dockyard, while I was steering the redhead away from her probing questions about plays, the theatre, Jimmy O'Dea, Hilton Edwards and all the rest, of which I knew absolutely nothing. In fact, I didn't even know where the Abbey was. The nearest I ever got to plays was when I used to listen to actors acting out a play on Radio Éireann every Sunday night with my mother while she toasted bread on the open coal fire for the nine of us, while my father used to be out drinking pints of Guinness.

Anyway after a few hours, the excitement of my first meeting in a public house with a girl other than my sisters plus the aroma of her perfume, the heat of the open fire in the bar and of course the alcohol, I suddenly felt quite sleepy, and I then started to doze off and only for Stretch's intervention, I'm sure that I would have fallen flat on my face in front of the first women I had ever met. Anyway, I did remember making a date for 7pm outside the Commodore for the following Saturday night. Stretch then dragged me towards the ten past eleven boat back to base, and when I arrived in the billet, I got into the bunk fully clothed and immediately fell asleep and very happily dreamt of my first date.

The "Doc" in Action

But it was back to reality the next morning, with PO

"Rommel" Scannell on duty. He walked with a slight limp, but my God, how he kicked our beds that morning at seven, it was inhuman. Here I was with my first hangover and he screaming "get up you lousy lot". Another new recruit, who had just joined up the previous day, said "shut fucking up, you bog trotter, and let me have some rest". "It's Sunday morning, don't you fucking know?" Scannell replied. "You'll be back where you came from my boy, on Monday morning, and then you an sleep all day everyday for all I care". It was back to routine duties again. The washhouse and breakfast that I couldn't touch for the first time in my life, and then into the No 1 uniform for mass parade, and the exact routine which I explained earlier except this time, the Batt Sullivan was outside the church selling the *Ireland's Own* and while inside, he was reading the jokes and then laughing at them, and then telling them to the organ player and singers who were preparing to perform at the rear of the church. All this was happening while mass was in progress. The naval chaplain I am sure must have been aware of the most unusual CPO Batt Sullivan.

When the mass finally ended, everyone automatically stood up, and then the CO and his family walked out, followed by the 2IC and his family and when they had well cleared the church, the remainder of the congregation also left. Outside the church, looking half dead from the cold and standing against the wall were cooks Dunworth and Billy Barry dressed in their No 1 uniforms, with no overcoats. "Why are you standing out here and not attending mass?" we asked. "Oh", said Dunworth, "we are just making a point. We were ordered by the duty PO to join the church parade, but when we arrived down, we refused to go in, even though he threatened us with the guardroom". "Fuck that", said Doyler. "There were two fucking Protestants, and another few non-believers, plus a few half-wits sitting in that centrally heated place for the past three quarters of an hour, and it didn't bother them one bit. So why didn't you two simply follow the others in and just watch them all praying?" I asked. "Well", they said, "we were only making a point".

"And what gave you that bright idea?" Stretch said. "The lawyer Barney". "And where's he? Up in Cork on a dirty weekend with a pass signed by "Wong". "Ah, fuck him too", replied Muxer, who was standing listening nearby.

After all that crap talk we slowly headed back up along the base and then we decided to visit the Doc who was on duty in the hospital, as he liked to call it. He spotted us from the window, and immediately ran outside to explain to us that unfortunately, he was unable to invite us inside for tea, because he was treating a seriously ill patient from the married quarters. "What's her name?" demanded Muxer. "We apply strict doctor-patient confidentiality in this hospital, and that's our policy, so clear off up to your billets", the Doc angrily demanded. "You're no fucking doctor, you twit", answered Hector. "You're only a medical orderly, and a poor one at that". "I'm the only doctor available here when the doctor from Collins Barracks is tied up in surgery". "You're only a prick", said Chippy Meehan. Unknown to us all, Muxer had slipped into the back window of the building for a quick look around for the "patient", and lying on the couch, stripped from the waist up, in the real doctor's room, was the very desirable, very sexy, young slim and beautiful wife of a married sailor, then living on the island. Muxer whispered his golden find to us and Meehan then said "What are you treat her for?" "Depression", answered the Doc "Go away you dirty fucker" said Muxer "you don't half strip a woman for that complaint, and you better not try to stick a tail into her, because her husband is mad jealous of her, and for telling us such a fucking lie, I'm going straight up to him to report you, and fuck you too!" continued Muxer "OK, lads", conceded the Doc "if I show you some good photos I took of her while changing into her swimsuit last summer down at the swimming pool, would you lot keep quiet?" "OK", we agreed, "it's a deal".

The Navy's Fleet

They were of course brilliant, and it must be added that her lovely developed body was very photogenic indeed, and his workmanship revealed every detail. The photos were such a success that we were force back to further threaten him with a report to the CO to force from him the negatives to be mass produced for general distribution within the entire service. After all that wheeling and dealing and threatening, it was back again to the dining hall for a dull dinner of corned beef and green cabbage that resembled grass, and probably was, if it were to be analysed. The dessert was jelly and custard, my favourite, which Larry O'Toole had ruined by turning it into a soup after placing the entire container onto the hot stove and melting the lot.

After that disastrous Sunday lunch, we again returned to the billets when I finally decided to bring up the subject of ships, for I didn't have a clue about how many we possessed, what type we had, or how large they were, and I still thought to myself that if the fleet was big enough, and when I eventually became an officer, I could, with a little luck and determination, captain my own vessel with perhaps a few hundred men under my command with the usual foreign voyages obviously thrown in. So here goes! I said to Muxer as casually as possible, "how many ships have we got? Well, I know we have a good few. Weren't you on one last night, half pissed with that long fucker, Joe Stretch?" "But that's only a passenger boat", I said. "It's a fucking ship of 93 gross tons, and has a horse power of 200, and she's only 53 years old. The Brits left her behind". "She must have been rightly fucked, if they didn't want her", added Willie Mynes. "OK, lads", I said, "what else have we, what about the warships?" At this stage, the remainder of the others were beginning to become very interested. "Look", insisted Muxer you asked about what bleeding ships we have, and I'm telling you, so shut fucking up. Next, there is the General McHardy, another steam job, and only 28 years old, and the Brits wouldn't take her either". "She must be a right heap of shite if they didn't want her", McGrane shouted from the billet on the other side. "Next, we have the motor vessel, John Adams, which is just 22 years of age and we use her for bringing army food up for us from Cork every Thursday. Down here it's called the ration boat". "How do you know all that info?" shouted Dermo Deeney, across to Muxer "I have it all written down, I got everything down in the transport hut last week". "Have we any battleships, cruisers, aircraft carriers or destroyers?" I then asked very impatiently. "Shut fucking up you, Brady. You asked what ships we have and I'm telling you, you bollocks". But they're only boats for passengers and civvies". "They are all owned by the Department of Defence. So shut fucking up, you cunt". "A cunt is useful and don't forget that", Hector said, while looking at everyone present. "Then we have the motor launch, the Sir Cecil Romer built in 1929 and she is 10 tons". "A 110 tons?" asked Cider. "No, 10 tons. We also have the M/L Raven, seventeen and a half tons, and two years older, plus the jackdaw, only 21 years old, but she weighs just seven and a half tons". "Fuck this", said Meehan, "how many more rowing boats have we got?" "Shut up, you Chippy, you can't even drive a nail into a piece of wood", answered Muxer "We also have the oil barge, Chowl, with a 50 horse power diesel and that is 100 tons in weight, but she's so old the records have never been found". "And don't forget to tell him about the CO's launch, the Colleen", shouted Georgie Long. "Now will you for Christ's sake, please tell me about all the warships, their size, their weight, and how many guns they carry? And what about the destroyers, are they fast? How many do we have? Could a few of them knock out a cruiser if they surrounded her, or put up a good fight? Does anybody know the names of any of our admirals? Has anybody seen any or even heard of them? So go on tell me everything". Hector, screaming with laughter, replied that the only admiral he had ever heard of was Nelson, and shouting over the howls of laughter from the others, said "all of our ships are falling apart, and should have been melted down years ago". "You mean the passenger ships for going ashore?" "No you ghoul, the fucking warships as you called them, are only a heap of shite". At this stage, the place was in uproar. "But how many have we?" "Eleven, including the Chowl". "But how many naval vessels?" "Three, and they are from the last war". "Oh my God", I answered, almost falling off the bed. "Did you say three altogether or three in dry dock?" "One-two-three", said Muxer pointing to his fingers. "Can you not count?" mutton head, Deeney roared through the laughter in the room. "Are you fuckers really serious?" I said almost sick, since my dreams were shattering all around me.

How can I ever be anything in a navy with three broken down ships to support me. "I must get out immediately and join the Royal Navy", I quickly decided to myself. But then on the road back home they will think of me as a failure. I then decided to stay here for a while and anything could happen, maybe even another world war, and then that lot in Dublin, whoever they might be, would be forced to buy proper warships to fight off the enemies. Stretch, sitting nearby quietly said to me that he heard somewhere that all we had was three ships. "And you wouldn't tell me, and now I have walked myself right into the shit with the rest of them!" "You never asked", he replied. "If you don't believe us Brady", Muxer continued, clearly enjoying himself now with the rest of them obviously on his side, "the numbers of the ships are 01, 02 and 03, and they are called the Macha, the Maev, and Cliona, and the officer down in the seamanship class told a friend of mine that all three were names out of mythology". "What's fucking mythology?" asked Cider. Nobody answered, but everyone sure had a puzzled look on their faces, and I bet mine was even more so. "Anyway", said Muxer "has any of you gobshites ever heard of Queen Maeve, or Macha or even Cliona?" The place was now in complete silence for the first time in about two hours. "Well, have you?" Nobody answered. "Well neither have I, you crowd of fucking gobshites".

I just lay on the bunk completely numb, unable to think or talk, and as the time dragged on, I couldn't even hear the remainder of their conversation, if that's how you could describe it. Here were my hopes and dreams absolutely shattered. What was I to do, desert and run away as a boy seaman on a tramp steamer, and see the world? But unfortunately, I overheard someone in the wet canteen saying that tramp steamers were crewed by queers, and the reason that they were that way was because they were away from women for long periods. Then I remembered that girls were more suited to my liking, and I began thinking about the redhead ashore in the Well House pub, the way she stared at me as if she really like me, and the shape of her breasts through her blouse, and the formation of her lovely legs. But those three ships kept haunting me. What use are three navy ships to an island race, stuck out in the Atlantic ocean? What if one is being repaired, and the likes of another Hitler decided to move in with battleships and aircraft carriers to kill us all and take over the entire country, north and south, Protestants and Catholics?

So then I roared over to the others in the room, "how big are our ships, and have they big guns that could stop modern fighting ships?" Paddy Smith then interjected, "look here", he said, "they carry rifles on the ship to threaten foreign fishermen, if they try to come near Ireland to steal our fishermen's fish". "Why's that? asked Stretch, "do they own them?" "Shut fucking up, you, Stretch", demanded Muxer "and you might learn something". "The ships have another fairly large gun called a four inch. I don't know why it's called that, because it's much bigger than that. Now they never fire it, because we are afraid we might hit something, and then they might hit back and sink us because the ships are rotting. Now at the middle of the ship, there are two 20mm anti-aircraft machine guns also from the last war, and they are only for show and are also never fired. At the rear of the vessel there is fitted a two pounder, but I know that's also heavier than that because I saw it down in a white-washed semi derelict shed last month. Down there, they were calling it a Pom-Pom" "That's more like the name of a lollipop or an icepop".

I just couldn't listen to any more of this extremely painful and stupid talk, so I decided to go down to the lower arch billet and lie on somebody else's bunk who was ashore. Except for myself, the room was entirely empty, and since the place was so quiet, I decided to switch on their radio to keep my mind off what I had just heard upstairs. After a few moments heating up the radio came on, and unbelievably the first song it played was *Ain't That a Shame*, sung by Fats Domino, which was a huge hit the previous year. Then I thought to myself, how the bloody hell did he know what I was going through and as the tears ran down my cheeks, I dozed off until the others, returning from a football match woke me up for tea. Thinking about the old ships I didn't notice what I was eating, and I cannot recall any other event inside the dining hall that evening. What I do remember, however, is standing outside the canteen, waiting for it to reopen at 6pm in order to remove the hunger and attempt to regain some weight loss.

Polishing Their Organs

Afterwards, Stretch, Doyler, and myself went upstairs for a few hours' snooker playing on a very excellent table, which was the finest piece of equipment that I have seen since I arrived in this terrible prison type place. After we tormented ourselves attempting to play a difficult game professionally, we eventually returned to the canteen for more mugs of tea and depth charges to keep us from starving to death while we slept. It was nearly eleven when we reached the billet and the radio was still switched on and on high volume with nobody listening to it, and as we were whitening our belts and our gaytors, the crowd from ashore were drifting in through the drill shed and making a lot of noise, walking on the wooden floor especially the culchies, who I was beginning to notice loved wearing the dreadful armys' heavy boots.

The terrible twins, two young recruits who went everywhere together, walked in and without a word, opened their kit boxes, removed what was needed for the next day's drilling and then brought everything down to the washhouse for inspection and touching up. Then both of them as if it was rehearsed filled up a sink with scalding hot water. Then they dropped their pants and from their towels, produced a large block of dark brown soap, the type my mother washed our floors with, then proceeded to drop their penises and testicles into the boiling water and scrubbed the hell out of them. I simply stood there unable to say or do anything. I was expecting their sexual organs to fall off and then be washed down the sink and away out to sea. After about fifteen minutes of this polishing and scrubbing and, of course, the closest of inspections, I finally couldn't wait any longer to ask them "what the fuck are you two up to? Do you pair not like what nature provided you with or are you changing your sex to a woman's?" "No", they said, "we're just after being with two fucking whores in Cobh, and we're afraid of our shite that we've got a dose from them and a doctor once told me to make sure you sterilise it after you have dipped it into someone you weren't sure of. And now, I won't be able to sleep tonight, thinking that if it has a big knob on it in the morning, I'm really in trouble because then it's straight to the doctor in Cork for a course of penicillin injections, and then hope for the best. Let's hope we didn't get a dose of VD from that dirty fucking bitch", added the pair of them. "It serves ye right", said Jack from Kerry, and he added with a roar as he ran up the stairs "he who dips his wick must pay for the oil". "Go away, you thick cunt", they replied with very worried expressions on their faces.

I'm Hauled Before "Hock"

I finished my equipment as quickly as possible, as I wanted to be as alert as possible for the next day when we would be drilling with our rifles for the first time, and according to the other trained recruits, we would also have to learn how to strip down and assemble the weapon until we could do it automatically, even when blindfolded. Monday morning came and after washing and then breakfast, we proceeded back to the billet and waiting for me was one of our instructors, Trooper O'Shea, who looked in terrible humour. "You, Brady, are really in the shite this time, you fucker". "How?" I asked. "You will soon find out. Report to the training office after parade, and you better have a good story ready, and you are good at making them up, aren't you, you gobshite?" Then he shouted, "everyone fall in". In the drill shed he was still staring at me. Ferriter then marched in with a rifle in the marching position up to his left shoulder, and dressed immaculately. He also kept staring at me, even when he was screaming out the orders in Irish to us. "Rinn Aire! Shasige Arash! Go Rare Clay! Go Maher Ma Shawl! Stad! Clay Umpig!" "Now, we're going out on that square in front of everybody and you, Brady, better not move an inch". "No, Sir", I answered as smartly as I could. "If you fucking move, Sonny." Then he started coughing and sneezing, "I'll march you around that square all day until you drop". All the others were standing stiffly to attention and looking straight ahead, and after parade, "the training officer wants to see you about a very personal matter, and be in your No 1 uniform". Jesus I thought, they are going to promote me or fuck me out. "All right then you lot", roared Ferriter, "Stand by for the square". "Rinn Aire! Go Rare! Clay go Maher Ma Shawl! Clay Cosaig! Das Cosaig! Clay Das! Rinn Stad! Clay Umpig! Shas Iag Arash! Air Huckrig! Then the 2IC and the chaplain arrived together and took up their positions with all the junior officers, lined up to their left. Then the warrant officer Nick Kennedy, equivalent to an army sergeant major, in a strong and clear voice ordered "Broad Aire!" and everyone stood stiffly to attention. He saluted the senior officer present, Petie Kavanagh, and reports the number of officers and ratings who were present. Next, the 2IC ordered "Broad! Shas Iag Arash! Air Huckrig!" Following that he demanded "Capina Dieg!", or something like that meaning "Remove your Caps". Then the chaplain started the prayers with words like "Oh Lord please grant calm weather to our sailors, and help them in their peril". Hector continued from behind me in the second row "and Jesus help us if we're sent out on those ships!"

When the praying and talking in the ranks finished, we were marched back into the drillshed and when Ferriter spotted me he yelled "Brady, fall fucking out. The remainder as you are. L S O'Shea, take over the class for rifle familiarity". So this is it, I murmured to myself. They are going to crucify me for something I bet I didn't do, or even know about. "Right", Ferriter ordered "get into that office fast". Inside, Hock was sitting smoking a Churchman cigarette with a lovely coal fire burning beside him. When he saw the two of us marching in, he asked Ferriter to leave the room, as this was a very delicate and personal matter, which he only wanted to discuss with me. I could read the expression of hurt and disappointment on Ferriter's face, and then I wondered why everything was so secretive. "Sit down, Brady", he said sharply. "I wish to have a private word with you about a young girl you were in company with ashore last Saturday night". "But, Sir I didn't lay a finger on her". He then replied, "We know that, it's just that her mother is an ex-girlfriend of mine and I went to school with her father back in Kildare, and she is very innocent, you know". "Well, Sir", I replied, "she didn't seem too innocent to me, with all her talk about being abroad in England for several years, and acting so confidently". "Ah yes", Hock said, "about acting, you told the girl you were an actor, now how can you be an actor, when you cannot even walk or speak properly?" "I am really trying, Sir". "That's not good enough. We want men of strong character and some ability and you have none of these, indeed Brady we are extremely doubtful about you, and we feel that you are incapable of ever passing through training division. In fact you are useless, useless to yourself, and useless to the service. "But Sir how did she know my name, because I never told her?" "It was quite simple you fool. I often go ashore to visit her mother and father, and sometimes she would be present, and I, of course, always wear my light boots, similar to those you were wearing in the Well House public bar. Now who was that other bloody fool you were with?" "Stretch, Sir". "Who?" "John Joseph Lynch". "Get out there and get him in here right away". "Yes, sir", I replied as I marched as smartly as possible out of the room. Outside Ferriter was standing against the wall smoking his pipe, and when he spotted me he very politely asked what was going on inside between myself and the training officer. "Well, Sir, Chief", I answered, "a TD has made representation to the CO for me to be considered as an Officer Cadet, and he has simply asked would I be interested, and now he wishes to speak with recruit John Lynch". "Brady, you'll never pass out of training division mark my words, and if you ever do, it will be in a wooden box, with me leading the parade". "Thank you very much Sir", I added.

Now, where I wonder is that other half, Lynch? After a few minutes I found Stretch in the toilet under the arch billet, and told him that Hock wanted to see him without delay. I then knocked at his door and walked straight in. Ferriter was present, and Hock nodded to him to leave the room. "Sit down you two", he ordered, and then offered us both a cup of coffee and a Churchman which we readily accepted. "Lynch", he commenced, "I have just explained to your fellow recruit that you are to keep clear from the two young ladies that you were chasing in Cobh last week, and if you do so there could be a bright future for the pair of you in the service , and if not well anything could happen. Do you know what I mean?" "Yes, perfectly, Sir", I answered. "Now, it's 'Stand Easy' time so go and have your tea break". "Yes, Sir and thank you Sir", we both replied. On our journey up to the canteen, we decided to consult with the lawyer without further delay. Inside the canteen he was in company with his two cronies Homan the 'Pigeon', and cook Dunworth. We then both said speaking together "Barney, we require some very technical advice immediately, and without delay", Stretch added. "OK" Barney agreed.

"Order me two cakes , a ham sandwich with mustard, and a bar of plain Cadburys chocolate, and a mug of tea, oh, and ten Players, and I'll speak to you at my bunk space at one fifteen. And be there, because others also require my assistance". "Isn't he getting very cocky?" remarked Stretch. "Yes", I agreed, "he's a bit of a know all, but please remember that we need him for the time being, and Stretch, don't forget the old saying, 'old soldier, old shite, young soldier, gobshite" "Yes", he agreed, we'll have to wait until after dinner before we make our next move".

We then turned to Hano and asked him "what's next on the training detail?" "We are all to fall in inside the drillshed at a quarter to eleven for stripping down the rifle". We then collected the weapons from the security of their racks in the billet and walked over to the drill-shed, where Hock, Ferriter and the Trooper O'Shea were waiting to speak to us. I watched Hock until he finally moved away from the NCOs and when I saw my chance I moved immediately. I saluted him as well as I could, and said "Excuse me Sir, may I ask you how you were able to identify Lynch and myself as the two who were in the company of the two young women ashore?" "Well, Brady", he said, "you two were easily recognised from the description they gave to their parents. One was said to resemble a clown dressed in nearly all the colours of the rainbow, wearing naval service boots and stockings, while the other twit, Lynch, would be spotted a mile away with that haircut, and he is shaped like a Hock, a fucking lamppost with no shape or make. Oh, that reminds me, Brady, go up to the base barber and tell him that I said you need a good tight and clean military haircut and I'll check his work personally myself first thing tomorrow". That remark I assumed, was to ensure that I would be unable to go ashore to meet that delicious and sexy looking redhead the following Saturday night, and when I meet Barney later, I'll also bring that up if I had time. "OK, Brady, is everything quite clear?" "Yes, Sir".

Detailing the Weapon

"CPO Ferriter carry on with the Lee-Enfield instructions". "Right away, Sir", answered Ferriter "L S O'Shea!" Ferriter roared, "Bring me a table and rifle from the training office and be smart about it". "Right away, Chief". The Trooper arrived back with the gun and a card table covered in green cloth similar to that which covers a snooker table. "Right", said Ferriter holding the rifle in his left hand, and pointing with a pencil he commenced explaining the various parts of the weapon and how it operates. "First, we have the butt. It's wooden as you all can see, and in case ye are too stupid to know, that's the part you press against your right shoulder (even if you are left handed) to fire it. Right at the end of the butt there is a lever which you can open very easily and inside you will find this, and while removing it", he explained, "this is known as a pull through for cleaning your rifle before and after firing. As you fools can see it's simply a piece of strong twine with a piece of brass at one end to act as a weight. That part is inserted into the barrel of the weapon and on the other end, a piece of soft cloth dipped in oil is pulled through. Now, is that perfectly clear?" Everybody answered "Yes, Sir" "The barrel is the steel part at the top where the bullet comes out. Now, could that be any simpler?" "No, Sir". Still pointing with the pencil, he explained "the trigger and around that, the trigger guard, and then the bolt, and in case any of you fools still haven't noticed, it's a bolt action weapon. So when you pull the trigger, it activates the bolt, and on the head of the bolt, a small pin strikes the shell of the bullet and then the powder within explodes and the .303 calibre bullet leaves the gun. Now, the weapon itself weighs nine pounds, and its overall length is 3 feet 9 and a half inches and with the bayonet fixed it's 4 feet 5 inches". It is the mark 2 version of the Lee-Enfield in case there's any doubt, and this is the magazine which is spring loaded to feed the ten rounds which it holds into the gun, and of course, there is a safety catch fitted. Now is that perfectly clear?" "Yes, sir", everyone again answered. Only then did I realise that he was reading the instructions from a British army handbook. "Take over, L S O'Shea, and teach those thicks, especially Brady and Lynch, how to strip and assemble their firearms back to front, because we are firing them on the range in Fermoy next week". "Right", the Trooper said, "pay attention". "To remove the magazine, you press very firmly the catch beside it. Then you take out the bolt. To move the bayonet, you turn it to the right, until you hear the click, and to remove it from the rifle, you press that catch, and turn it in the reverse order. To load the magazine, you place the rounds side by side, ensuring that they are not entangling, and are all facing the right direction, and so forth", until we could master the art of cleaning and maintenance, plus the stripping and assembling blindfolded. "Finally", he said, "alright, it's lunch time, off you go", but it's parade again at 1.45". I couldn't wait to see Barney, even through that very interesting time learning about the rifle. I was wondering what his directions might be, and what the others were going to say or think. Either way, I thought, I'm in for a good slagging, and that's for sure.

After a dinner of stew, and believe me it was Irish, well certainly Irish naval stew and flavour, and it was difficult to trace the meat, I immediately complained to the chef, and was told quite positively that the meat was always well boiled into everything and was therefore untraceable. After we finished with that lot, we rushed up to the billet, where Barney was waiting for us with a sheet of paper and a fountain pen in his hand. "Now, we'll all sit on my bed", he said, "and start at the beginning and tell me everything and leave absolutely nothing out". We hated having to go through telling him about he women in particular, because we felt that was private, and by telling him, the entire base would know in a very short period of time. Anyway, we started and explained how we met the girls, and what was said, and about my next date on Saturday night. "Now, what the fuck did you want to see me about?" "Barney", I said, "you asked to hear everything". "OK, what's bleedin annoying you then?" "Well", Stretch continued, "Hock found out about us through their parents, and he warned us to lay off them". "And were you actually on them?" Barney asked. Thunder overheard that remark and quickly shouted for all to hear "I'm sure that pair of dirty fuckers tried". "OK, you lot", shouted Barney, "this interview is none of your shagging business, so lay off. Alright", said Barney, as he began to become impatient, "what did Hock say?" "Well", I said, "if we leave them alone, there could be a bright future for both of us and if we didn't, then anything could happen to us". "That's a load of bollocks", answered Barney. "He has no hold over you once you go ashore, and if you get into trouble while over there, well, that's a police matter, and if I were you, I would have told that Hock to go and fuck himself!" "Go away you, Barney", said Joe Barr from Derry, with a look of contempt on his face. "If Hock even looked at you, you would shit yourself".

We were then ordered out for more square bashing, this time with the Lee-Enfield rifles. The arms drill is reasonably easy if only we could have understood those damn Irish commands. I must stress that at that time, nobody down from the commanding officer, ever thought of telling anybody in any class, the English translation, because for instance, you then would have known that you were supposed to start marching or walking, leading always with the left foot, and that a simple explanation to explain that "Clay Das!" meant "left, right!" That way, I am positive we would have learned much quicker, since we would have understood the language. Anyway, we learned fairly quickly how to slope arms, order arms, present arms, and lay down the weapons in line with the toe of your right boot. To my ear, the Irish versions of the above orders sounded something like this: "Clionag Arms! Seehig Arms! Togig Arms! Tarragig Arms! and Lagieg Arms!, without of course, an Irish version for arms.

A Haircut Military Style?

During a short break in the billet for cleaning and oiling the rifle, I asked the others what qualifications had the barber. Mynes said "Just look at Stretch's head, and you'll soon find out". "Yes", Barney said, continuing, "that's because Stretch is so bleedin mean. If he had handed the barber a few bob before he started butchering, he would have given him a decent haircut, something you wouldn't have been afraid to go ashore with". "So, if I pay him when I go up, he won't destroy me?" "Yes, you gobshite!" Barney answered. "The more you give, the better the haircut job, it's as simple as that". "And where's the barber's shop?" "Up the hill somewhere behind the CO's house. On your way, don't be caught looking into the officer's quarters, because the last peeping tom, Considine, did six weeks in detention for spying on Lt Sullivan's lovely sexy daughter, who was sunbathing topless in her back garden. So watch yourself, Brady". "OK, but how much will I give him?" "Well, if I were you (and I hope I never will be) I would drop two bob into his hand, and don't say a word, just pretend it's not bribery, which it is. And another thing, he is getting paid by the taxpayer for cutting your hair, and do you know, six pence is stopped every week for our haircuts, and then we have to pay him again out of our own pockets, otherwise he destroys us, and then we can't go out for weeks. The Mafia are only in the half penny place here", he added.

I made my way up slowly to the barber's shop in order to kill as much time as possible, and as I strolled past Lt Grennall's home, his lovely wife said "Hello, are you looking for something?" I was too frightened to even look at her after what the lawyer, Barney, had told me about Considine. So I just walked past until I came to another of those semi-derelict buildings of which Haulbowline island is infamous for, and the sign outside the whitewashed construction simply said "Barber". When I entered I couldn't help noticing that he was using a hand operated shears of the type my father used to use on myself and my two brothers, before I joined this place. The other equipment which Tom had at his disposal, was a filthy mirror, presumably to inspect his professional work on yourself as you left; a sink with just one large brass tap; a leather for sharpening the cut throat razor; a bar of soap; a dirty towel; two combs; two scissors; and a large and heavy electric shears, which he started to operate a few moments after I arrived. The unfortunate who he was working on was in a terrible mess, and he obviously hadn't bothered to offer the Barber anything for his technical ability. Tom the barber was simply running the monster of the machine right up the sides and back of the chap's head with simply no thought of style or of what condition he was likely to leave his client. It was just terrible to watch, so there and then I instantly decided to press a two and sixpenny piece into Tom's hand when the other three who were sitting on the bench before me were (in my eyes) literally finished. I was watching Tom's alarm clock as it ticked away for I had it figured out that I would skip the remainder of the afternoon on this trip. My time came and I quickly handed over the bribe which was accepted without any expression of gratitude, but thankfully, when the operation was completed, my head was in reasonable condition, and now all that was on my mind was to return to my quarters and change my clothes because the hairs down my neck were driving me mad with the itch.

A Feast in the Billet

Shortly after tea one of the recruits mentioned to us in the billet that the ration boat, the John Adams, which I mentioned here earlier, was doing an extra run from Cork to Haulbowline, and back again the following day, and since there was a crew shortage, himself and another lad were detailed to give a hand loading and unloading, and that according to the other fellow, who was an AB, it was dead easy to rob food when the civilian crew were down below having tea. "All you need", he told the recruits, "is a small kit bag or a gas mask holder, and when they are not looking, stuff everything into them and then cover the lot with a towel". The pair of them headed off the following morning, at 8 am and, obviously, the topic of conversation all day was what would they return with. Then at 5pm, they marched in with the goods, and emptied everything out onto the floor. Included were four chickens, around six pounds of beef sausages, approximately the same amount of butter, and a big wrap up of black and white pudding, liver, kidneys, and a couple of dozen large eggs, plus a tin of beef, they called kosher, large tins of tomatoes, beans and peas, and a large selection of fresh vegetables. The recruit also had stuffed down his trousers (but wrapped well in grease proof paper) four pork steaks, and two T-bone steaks, he confessed were stolen for himself and his accomplice from the special rations set aside for the CO and his sidekick, Kavanagh and another officer they called "Spaghetti".

That evening we got ready for the feast because believe me, we were starving and we were determined that we were going to enjoy this lot all in one go, by hook or by crook. We collected enough money between us for the gargle and cider was the obvious buyer in this regard, so he was detailed to buy as much Bulmers as was humanly possible with the amount we could afford, and if any cash was left, then try to purchase twenty Players or Gold Flake, even ten would do, since we would divide them between us all. I was ordered down to the cookhouse to soften up my townie, Larry O'Toole for the loan of a small frying pan and some dripping, and Muxer shouted as I left "If he has no dripping, ask him to skim some off the top of tomorrow's soup, that will do". Then Barney said "Any port in a storm". I returned with the pan, plus a cup full of the fat that found its way to the top of the soup. When the canteen opened, Cider rushed in and ordered eight flagons of Bulmers and with the change he bought a large bottle of Guinness and ten Gold Flake, and returned immediately to the billet. Muxer went over to the coal yard beside the NCO's Mess and filled two buckets while nobody was looking. Everything was then hidden in the yard under the arch billet until after the Duty Officer's Rounds at 9pm. At 9.10pm exactly, Lt "The Yank" Mahony walked through and remarked to all of us "Isn't anyone going ashore then?" We answered "No, Sir, we have decided to stay back and clean up our kits for tomorrow". He didn't answer, and walked down the steps and across the road and into the main billets.

Now that the coast was absolutely clear, the stove was stoked up, goodies were removed from their hiding place, and the greatest feed that I ever received while I was based down there was about to begin. The frying pan was placed onto the red roaring fire and then the soup topping was poured from the cup which contained more soup than fat, but nobody really noticed, since we recognised everything there as live-saving food. The sausages were thrown on first, and before any of them were given any chance to turn brown, Halligan scooped out a handful and placed them between two thick slices of pan bread which had been removed from the supply stores earlier, right under the nose of the assistant, the excellent Tony Fahy The pudding, rashers, eggs, even the liver and kidneys were devoured in the same savage manner, and of course, the beans and peas, plus the Italian tinned tomatoes were eaten cold and removed from their containers with our issue knives and forks. A huge pot of tea was then brewed with a tin plate used as a cover, and believe me, it was so strong, we nearly had to spoon it out, it was similar to treacle. To round off the evening, we switched on our radio. Whatever station we picked up, it was broadcasting smashing songs, two of which I thought were very appropriate, *Sixteen Tons* by Tennessee Ernie Ford (that reminded me of Mynes, loading and unloading the boat earlier in the day) and Dean Martin singing *Memories are Made of This*.

After a while listening to the current hits on the radio, Doyler then removed the accordion from his specially reinforced kit box and played a few tunes. We sang along, ensuring that we kept our voices down and that all windows were tightly closed, for the officers' quarters were very near, and we didn't want to alarm them to the fact that we were thoroughly enjoying ourselves as a group for the first time since our arrival. Lots more coal was added to the stove, and then Cider was instructed to rescue the alcohol from its secret hiding place, and to divide that and the cigarettes equally. Stretch, as usual, declined the alcohol, but he requested (and received) two cigarettes in lieu. We switched off all lights at exactly 12 midnight, and sat around the now red coloured pot bellied steel stove, spoke and joked, obviously about the women we knew ashore. As the Bulmers flowed, we generally fucked from a height every officer we knew, and Ferriter. We finally hit the beds at around twenty to three, and believe me, everybody slept like new born babies that night, and we woke up at 7am that morning fresh and rearing to go well satisfied with ourselves. That was one method we used to survive. I will explain others at a later stage.

Hock never pulled me up about my haircut, so I assumed it looked OK. Then I forgot about the event.

A Change in Appearance

The next few days passed off fairly quickly with nothing happening out of the usual. Then, thank heavens, Friday came around again, and another two pounds and nine pence. It wasn't much I know, but I was really waiting for it. This week, I had decided to get a pound postal order from Nan Coveney down in the base post office, and send it onto my mother. Since I was in desperate need of a new rigout, I was also going to enclose a note asking her to contact her Jew man friend, whom she used to get a loan of money from. I did remember he called to our house in a motor car every Saturday morning, with an attractive girl he called his assistant. My mother used to moan to my father about his high interest rates, but she always went to him when one of us needed new clothes for First Communion or Confirmation. Firstly I will ask her to press him for ten pounds. Then, I'll have to check the prices of clobbers up in Cork to make sure I had enough cash, although I did overhear someone down here saying that all men's shops in Cork only cater for farmers and hillbillies. We shall see when I secured the cash.

Meanwhile, I would have to figure something out for the next night, when I prayed that against all odds, that delicious little redhead would turn up at the Commodore! But first things first. What was I to wear? The No 1 uniform, despite being presentable, is too obvious no matter where you go, so that was out, and I couldn't leave this place in the get up that I wore the previous week. So, what was the alternative? I then decided to consult with my two right hand men, Stretch and Doyler. After half an hour's deliberation over lunch, consisting of smoked cod and peas, it was decided that I had no other option but to hire out an outfit from someone of my height and build in the service, and the gear would have to be fairly new and stylish. But who had purchased new clothes recently? We had to wait until the end of that day's training (Secure, as it's called). That evening the three of us searched every billet and spoke to everyone we knew, asking them who would have an outfit that would fit me. Finally, we were directed up to the Signal's billet on the top of the hill, and to ask for a fellow they called the Blusher, the lad who I already mentioned having noticed on the boat on my arrival. He said that in fact he had bought a new suit and overcoat the previous week, and that both were very expensive, but he refused to divulge the cost. I then asked to see the clothes and he immediately removed from a plastic covering, a lovely military style blue full length gabardine overcoat and a two piece blue serge suit. Both definitely smelled and looked new. I then, along with my two companions proceeded to the washhouse which is fitted with a number of mirrors. With their help and honest comments, I checked every angle and every movement as I modelled the garments, walking up and down, similar to models on a catwalk. After various remarks from my advisors, it was agreed that if the turnups on the trousers were dropped, then the pants would be a perfect fit, just resting on the shoes. Otherwise, everything was in good order.

Now, for the agreed price for an evening's wear! We haggled over a price for nearly three hours and by the end of that time, he had me almost worn out, despite the back up I was receiving from the other pair. His lowest price was ten shillings for the loan of the two items, because he said he would have to get them dry cleaned in Cobh after I had used them. I then said "Fuck you too!, my mother could buy me that lot for twelve bob". "Yes, that's right", said Stretch, "but you would be the laughing stock of the place". "OK", I finally said, "I'll pay you on Sunday morning". "Oh, no", the Blusher replied. "I want the cash up front, a ten bob note if you have it please". On the way back to the room, Stretch said, "he really robbed you, didn't he?" Doyler continued, "if she turns up and then if Hock catches up with you, you could desert in the gear, and fuck the Blusher". On the way down, we again visited the canteen, and Doyler ordered three mugs of tea, six depth charges, a box of matches, and an ounce of yachtsman plug tobacco. After that snack, he lit up his bent shank pipe and I again said to myself "he's turning into an old man overnight".

The "Doc's" Second Performance

As we were about to leave, the Salmon Poacher ran in screaming that Cider had collapsed inside the wet canteen, and that they thought he was dead because he was unable to move for ten minutes. I remembered the antique stretcher which I had noticed down in the so-called hospital. So Stretch, Doyler and myself rushed down for a loan of it to carry Cider down for immediate assistance. We were quickly followed by "Tiny" Little and Muxer, and when we reached the building, the front door was locked. But we were positive the place was occupied, for we could hear the radio in the background, and the lights were on in the office, plus the unmistakable aroma of bacon and eggs was coming from an open window. We rang the door bell, and banged the windows, but still he refused to answer. So Muxer without a moment's thought, rushed around to the rear window of the premises and looked into the same window as before, and noticed very clearly the Doc having intercourse with a lovely newly wed smashing young blond from the nearby married quarters. Muxer watched this erotic demonstration for as long as possible, until the Doc finally noticed the shadow at the window, and when he did, he almost died of fright. The Doc then immediately jumped up, put his pants on, pulled up the zip, which caught part of his penis on the way up, and as he screamed with pain, Muxer then shouted to him through the window "That'll keep you quiet for a good while, you dirty fucker!" He then walked slowly to the door and asked us what we wanted. "Well", Doyler answered, "not what she's getting! What are you treating her for?" "Anxiety", answered the Doc. "You don't even know what that word means", shouted Stretch. "Please don't tell anybody", he then pleaded, "because I'll be fucked out of here by the doctor if he finds out maybe even onto one of the ships, and I'm a bad sailor. I'd absolutely die at sea. Can't we work something out? I'll give you lot three pounds of sausages and a big lump of steak, and a bag of spuds if you keep your mouths shut about this". We then looked at one another and at once agreed because then our only real concern was for Cider, but only if he promised to remain overnight with the patient, since we believed it could have been more serious than a simple overdose of Bulmers.

We then returned to the wet canteen which was once the Royal Irish Constabulary Barracks, under the British, and removed Cider on the stretcher down to the gentle care and attention of the Doc, where he fully recovered the following morning, along with a murdering hangover. Thankfully, after all that hassle with the Blusher, Cider and that dirty fucker, the Doc (who, it appears, cannot keep his hands off any girl), we were glad that the next morning being the CO's rounds, there were no parades and the only work would be cleaning up for his inspection. This time, PO Cantwell detailed me to clean out the washhouse, including all the sinks, mirrors, and windows, and Chippy Meehan was ordered to clean the toilets and urinal. Stretch and Doyler were sent into the billet to sweep the floor and then wash it, and tidy up all the beds and make sure that there was no washing on the line, and that the steel stove was blackened and polished, and all ashes removed. All this was now becoming simple routine to the entire unit. When everything was completely satisfactory, Cantwell told us to get lost until after McKenna had passed through. Then back down to the civvy canteen for another feed with the usual crowd.

On our way back up the island, we noticed the massive outline of a huge passenger liner entering Cork harbour. Her gigantic height and width appeared to cover the entire entrance, and when her steam siren blew, the sound almost deafened us for a few moments. From her colouring and markings, plus the number of funnels she carried, it was obvious to Warrant Officer Kennedy that she was the SS United States, which along with other liners including the SS New York, and other famous transatlantic vessels were then very frequent visitors to this great deep anchorage, for the rich and not so rich, and famous to embark and disembark. Since this was obviously a big day in Cobh, Stretch, Doyler and myself decided to rush ashore in the first available launch which was again at ten past two. The SS General McHardy was the duty boat, and when we all went aboard her, I could see that by now, the boat was completely loaded to her regulation two hundred passengers, which was the maximum amount she was permitted to carry in fine weather. When we walked ashore, the main street was just like outside Croke Park after an all-Ireland game had finished. The town was jam packed and you could only move with the crowd. What immediately caught my eyes were the bright coloured and flashy clothes the yanks or returned yanks wore. They made them instantly conspicuous, and of course, their cameras were hanging around their necks with the lenses resting on their chests. The narrow roads were jammed with those large, ugly automobiles that were so popular in the 1950s, because in the United States, motor fuels were so cheap. Some had sun roofs but a lot of them had a large amount of chrome fitted around their bumpers, and most had car radios installed, which I had only seen for the first time. The entire deep water quay was sealed off by Customs Officers, and the station was packed with passengers and trains ready to take them to their destinations.

Then, as we looked out the liners tender was leaving the pier fully loaded with passengers and their luggage, and as it headed down river to the waiting liner, we could clearly observe the look of sorrow on the faces of those on deck, perhaps looking at Ireland for the last time. The most surprising memory of that period was that the liners' passengers spent so little time in the port, for within a couple of hours, the town was again very quiet and peaceful, except for the Cathedral's bells, which rang out every fifteen minutes. We again walked about Cobh, down Westbourne Place, past the old Rob Roy Hotel, then up to inspect the site of the pub on Harbour Row, where the great boxer, Jack Doyle was refused employment. We headed up West View to marvel at the extraordinary houses commonly known as "The Pack of Cards". Later, we checked out the former Admiralty House, then a nuns' convent, which was, during World War I, the Headquarters of Admiral Bayly, Commander-in-Chief of the coast of Ireland.

It started to rain, so we headed for the Sailors' and Soldiers' rest for an hour in their reading room, which was only equipped with uninteresting women's magazines that were over three months old. We then left to return to Haulbowline on the twenty to five boat to have our tea, and to get ready for the most important date with that darling of a redhead, who had promised to meet me at 8pm outside the Commodore Hotel. I wasn't very interested in the tea, for at that time my only concern was how would I handle the situation if she did turn up. For instance, would I tell her that my suit and overcoat were only hired out for the evening, or pretend that I had purchased them with part of the compensation I received from CIE for the loss of my luggage? Would I come clean and confess to here that I was not really an actor and could never be one? How would I manage things if she turned up with her mother, and if she reported me to the police who are stationed just a few doors up from the Commodore? Those real worries were still in my mind when I entered the washhouse that evening, and listening to Paddy Smith, Georgie Long and Brendan McGrane singing *Three Coins in the Fountain* made me think that this trio hadn't a care in the world. I showered, and tried again to shave, as I was convinced that a beard was beginning to grow. However, I do remember begging the use of Willie Myne's Old Spice aftershave lotion and a piece of Georgie's Brylcreem, which was then in fashion. I then secured the loan of a white shirt from "Pinhead" and a blue tie with white dots from Tom Kendrick. I tried on the entire outfit, with a loan of a pair of black shoes from Dermot Kelly. Stretch and Doyler pronounced me suitable for shore leave in the company of a beautiful lady.

With Ann in Cobh

Going out on the ten past seven launch, the General McHardy, I was nearly drunk with excitement and I could hardly talk to the others, for my mouth and lips were dry, and I kept repeating to myself "What the hell am I to say if she does turn up? What do I tell the crowd in the billet when I return later, because by now I am the talk of the place?" When we landed in Cobh we had a quick look around before going down to the Well House for a quick drink to calm my nerves before heading back up to meet her (I hoped!). Then at exactly five minutes to eight, I left to meet her, and on my way up, I kept repeating to myself over and over again "Keep calm, she will be there". As I reached English's Newsagents, I could make out the outline of a young woman, standing close to the Commodore and my heart began to thump harder and harder until I was convinced that it was about to burst. When, at last, I reached the hotel, she was indeed waiting, and her first words were "You are the greatest liar I have ever met! All that talk about being an actor, and then pretending to have been sent for by the Naval Service is all just rubbish, and you know it. Do you think that just because we live down here that we are all fools? And what's more", she continued, "Lt Hock told my father that not only were you a recruit over there, but you are the worst they ever had. Now why in heaven's name did you tell me so many stupid lies?" After such a dressing down I somehow stammered out that I was only trying to impress her because she looked and smelled so lovely that night in Andy's Well House Bar. I then pleaded with her to accompany me back down to Andy's for a few drinks, for I wanted to show her off to Hano, Cider, Stretch, and Doyler, whom I knew were still there drinking and playing darts. We just stayed for two drinks, because I was very keen to take her down to the Ormonde Cinema, which was situated between waste ground (where recreational accommodation was constructed during the First World War for American servicemen, who were stationed over here) and the public baths (where Irish Emigrants were washed and disinfected before being allowed on board ships sailing for America). As we entered the cinema, I was delighted to notice that the film being shown was 'High Noon', starring Gary Cooper, and another beautiful woman, Grace Kelly. Inside was reasonably comfortable, and as I sat down I thought to myself, here I am sitting beside a lovely girl, and very soon I would be watching another on the screen.

I then heard for the first time the most beautiful music being played throughout the cinema while we waited for the movie to commence. It was totally different to what I had so far encountered. So, I turned to my clever friend and asked her, "what form of music is that, and what would you say is the title of it?" "That", she instantly replied, "is classical music, and now you are listening to Tchaikovsky's Nutcracker Suite. I know, because we have it at home. It's a 78, and we often play it on the record player". She also identified the next piece of music, which was, according to her, Mendelssohn's Piano Concertos No 1 and No 2 and she further stated that according to Einstein, he was the romantic classicist. "Oh, I see", I replied, "and where did you learn that from?" "Well, it's written on the back of Mendelssohn's record sleeve. Now, Jim", she asked, "where did you get that lovely suit and overcoat?" "Well, to be perfectly honest, Ann" I said as casually as possible, "my mother wired down the money to me, and I immediately rushed up to Cork on the first train possible, because I was so eager to look my best because I was meeting you". "And was it expensive Jim?" "Yes, Ann", I replied, "very expensive, but it was worth every penny just to be sitting here with you".

Then the lights dimmed and the film commenced, and I held her hand firmly and my heart again started to thump as if I were in a marathon race. Then I reached across and kissed her soft lips, and Dermot Kelly, whom I didn't notice on my way in, kicked the back of my seat and shouted, "Straighten up, Brady, you're blocking my view". "That jealous fucker", I thought to myself, and just as I was getting started! Anyway, there will be other chances, when I will, without fail, take them with both hands. The presence of Kelly in the seat behind made me feel very uneasy, so I wasn't really sorry when the movie ended, and then we strolled back to Andy's which was packed with navy chaps and their girl friends, all getting drunk on the cheap, and I mentioned to Ann "How can this last with a man in his condition selling goods below costs, and even allowing some of his customers to serve themselves? He is bound to go broke very soon", I added as I walked her home, up Harbour Row. She told me that her father was a harbour pilot, and that he had achieved his captain's certificate with the Esso Oil Company, sailing on their ships for over twenty years. She added that sometimes, her mother sailed with him on the larger tankers while herself and her two sisters were in boarding school in Cork. "So that's where you got your good education!" She simply replied by asking me did I intend staying in Haulbowline and making a career out of it. "Well", I said, "the conditions and food over there are terrible, and some of the instructors are as ignorant as pigs, but overall I am being treated very reasonably, and I have signed up for six years, and no matter what, I have no intentions of deserting, because as far as I'm concerned, only cowards desert". As we reached her home, it was almost midnight, and the last launch left in ten minutes. So I held her soft body close to mine and again kissed her on the lips, and whispered to her, "Oh, my God, I wish I could stay with you tonight". As I was about to depart for the last launch back to base, I asked here where she worked and would it be possible to have her telephone number. She replied that she was employed in the main office of Fords in Cork, and that the telephone number was in the book, and to ring anytime except during lunch.

Then I ran all the way back down to the naval pier and jumped aboard as the military policeman was closing off the gangway. Muxer immediately spotted me and roared across the deck "Did you get it, or even get a feel of it?" Hector then replied "Don't mind him, he's just jealous". The remainder of the passengers, and the crew plus the red cap were unusually quiet that night, so I asked Hector "What's going on?" "Well", he said, "when the ten past ten launch was returning, a young seaman jumped overboard without saying anything to anyone. Then all of a sudden, someone shouted 'Man overboard on the port side!' The only officer on board, Lt "The Yank" Mahony rushed up to the bridge and ordered the captain to stop engines, because there was an emergency. He then took complete control and demanded that nobody dare follow the man who was now shouting and screaming for help in the harbour. Instead he directed that the launch be turned around, and a complete search be then undertaken. They combed the area for an hour before returning to Haulbowline, and then every boat that was available was called into the search, but the very strong currents had very quickly moved the body far away from the immediate area. The "Yank" had made the right decision", otherwise more lives would have been lost, and that was recognised at a later inquiry. The body was recovered, in a condition similar to jelly, at the mouth of the harbour, three weeks later, covered in crabs. He was then removed to the naval hospital by the "Doc" and others, on the canvas stretcher, which we had used for Cider the night he had collapsed. When the deceased's friends were interviewed by the military police, it was revealed that he had been very upset, due to a lover's quarrel with his girlfriend, who had told him that she was seeing another chap, and that she was therefore giving him up. He then proceeded to get drunk, and while going back on the boat he simply jumped over the side, without saying anything to anyone.

The following morning was Sunday, and church parade again, and the usual routine with the Batt Sullivan talking and reading the jokes out of *Ireland's Own*, while Rory McCarthy was trying to sing, and Teddy Murphy was attempting to play the organ. As I recall, that day was extremely wet, so we remained indoors and listened to and enjoyed our only luxury, the ever faithful radio, and because of our location, we were able to tune into very many stations indeed. Among the songs and tunes I remember hearing then were Frank Sinatra singing *Love and Marriage*; Julie London, *Cry Me A River*; The Platters, *Only You*; plus Mitch Miller, *Yellow Rose of Texas*.

The Army's Firing Range

After parade on Monday morning, CPO Ferriter announced to us in the drillshed that on the following Thursday, we were heading to Kilworth, near Fermoy, to fire the rifles on the army's range, and therefore in the meantime, we would be learning how to aim the rifles at the targets until we understood it inside out. So that routine continued right up to the appointed date, and at 8.30 on Thursday we were again ordered to collect our rifles from the billets, take our oilskins in case it rained, collect our sandwiches, mugs and tea boiler from the cookhouse, plus a sack of coal from the coalyard. The Doc was present with a full first aid kit in case anybody got (not too seriously) hurt. We were then marched down to catch the nine o'clock boat out, and as it pulled out, Sgt Joey Cummins trotted down after being informed that he might be needed to adjust some weapons during the firing drill. When we reached Cobh the army truck which was to take us up to Kilworth, was parked opposite, outside the Garda station and then we quickly loaded everything on board. Without delay, we headed off and before we reached Glanmire, most of us were getting sick out over the sides and back of the lorry, because of the strong fumes from the engine's exhaust system, which was entering through the wooden floor. Eventually, we reached the location, directly across from the military barracks and unloaded everything and walked across fields for about ten minutes until we reached the target areas. We then filled up sandbags to use for resting our rifles while we fired from the ground. Willie Mynes was then detailed to light the fire in the shed to boil the water for the tea, and then a field telephone was set up between targets, and the firing localities. Muxer myself, Stretch, Doyler, Jack Brennan and Tiny Little were ordered to the targets area. This place is situated in a dug out well below the targets, and when everything is ready for firing, the targets are then hoisted up on a steel rail, and into position for firing practice, as each contestant shoots at his chosen target. We then signal back with differed coloured boards with each colour identifying the various scoring points. For instance, a white board signalled back to the firing point means that you have scored a bull's eye, and a flag moved across the target from right to left shows that you have completely missed the target altogether. However, we waited willing and able for the firing to commence because after the first party had fired, we would break for tea and sandwiches, and then return to the firing line, and they then would mark the targets for us. So we waited for word on the telephone that the show was on, but instead Ferriter appeared, and ordered us back to the hut for our tea break instead. Word then started to filter out through the army truck driver that in fact the most important item (the ammunition) had been overlooked. What in fact had happened was that Ferriter who was so preoccupied with ordering us around, and making sure we didn't miss the boat out, overlooked the point that the officer was making his own way directly from Cobh without visiting Haulbowline on the way. Therefore, he also overlooked the fact that it was, his the officer's responsibility to have signed for the ammunition before we left.

Since we were literally up the creek it was decided that we should return to base, and again the trip was terrible with almost everybody on board being very sick. That evening, we were again informed that we would be heading back the next day to Kilworth, for another attempt at range practice. Again at the appointed time we left Cobh in the same smelly lorry and it rained very heavily throughout the journey, and by the time we reached the firing locality, we were unable to see the four foot targets at a range of one hundred yards. Therefore, Lt "Ski" Daly commanded that everyone eligible to fire should point towards the targets and commence firing until their two allocated magazines of bullets were used. By then, everybody was soaked to the skin and without delay, we rushed back to the transport, and returned to Haulbowline for pay, which was issued through the main office. Then after that we were obliged to perform a very important operation. The rifles must be thoroughly cleaned after firing, while the barrel is still hot, so we were told by Joey Cummins to boil as much water as possible and pour that water into all the weapons, in order to remove the dust and dirt from within the grooves inside the barrel. "Now lads he said, get your pull through, add a little oil to the four by two cloth and pull it through the barrel just once, then the gun is properly maintained and ready for firing whenever that may be". "And Joey, how did we do at the range today?" "Oh you all passed, some had very good scoring, Brady was only average".

A Bright Future?

Well, thank God all that was over, recruits' training was finally finished, but I still had those damn corn plasters all around both feet. Maybe now I might have a chance to rid myself of those horrible noisy and hard ugly hob-nailed so called boots. Since I was now out of that torture chamber called "Training Division", plus Hock and the terrible Ferriter I wondered hard and long about what branch of the service I would enter. Cooking didn't appeal to me because to start there, it's peeling tons of potatoes for weeks before you're let near a cooker, and then the slagging and bad humour directed towards you because of the food quality. So that was out. What about the seaman's division? Again, I thought long and hard because that involved a lot of deck duties in wet and cold weather, day and night on the ships, and there's too much dealing with officers while the ship is sailing as lookouts and as helms' men, so that too was definitely dead, as far as I was concerned. Now what about signals branch? Well I was sort of interested, but that lot reminded me of a pack of queers waving flags around and flashing lights, and funnily, what really put me off was that they were always too clean for my liking. Then, what was left? The main office badly needed personnel, but nobody would volunteer. I also disliked the idea of working as a medical orderly with the Doc on the rampage. I finally decided that the mechanical branch was more to my liking. Besides, I figured that there could be a highly skilled trade attached to it. So I applied to that section, and I was quickly accepted, perhaps too quickly, it appears.

The mechanical division was then housed back in the main billet, so I was therefore ordered to remove my kit and rifle to join the others which included several former colleagues from recruits and apart from Stretch, Hector, Hano, Cider, Hume, and Doyler, we were joined by Brockelbank, "Blinkey" and Willie Mynes. Immediately he spotted me, Blinkey told me that Ferriter wanted to see me in Hock's office right away. On my short trip across I wondered what he wanted me for. I knocked on Hock's office door, and walked straight in. Then Hock said, "Brady, we were afraid that you were never going to pass through the Recruit's Division, and in fact, we are delighted that you have done so well. Therefore, we have decided to present you with these two tickets, to see 'The Cruel Sea', presently showing in Cork. The prize is not for being the best recruit in the class, but for being the most improved". "Well, thank you very much Sir", I answered as smartly as a highly trained member of the Defence Forces could. "And tell me Brady, who do you intend taking to the Cinema to view that great sea story, which of course involves our class of vessels, the marvellous Corvettes, the backbone of the battle of the Atlantic? Don't forget, Brady, without them the war against Hitler's U-Boats would have been lost". "Well, Sir" I said, "my mother is travelling down by car especially to congratulate me on doing so well so far in the service and now, I have decided to take her along to see the picture which you have so highly recommended, and to see for herself what type of naval vessels her son will be serving on". "That's very thoughtful of you, Brady. Always look after your mother". "Thank you, Sir", I answered. "Alright", Ferriter said, "you are dismissed, you may return to your billet".

As I strolled back to the room, I wondered did that pair in the office really believe that my mother was coming down, and that she would be attending the cinema with me in Cork, because she had neither the time nor the money for such a luxury, since she was far too busy working part-time to supplement my father's very poor wage, which was quite inadequate to feed and clothe eight young and healthy children at home. My first and only choice for that treat was my lovely clever Ann, out in Cobh, but first I must figure out the arrangements for seeing her when I sort out my suit and overcoat, because I am not going to continue hiring them out or scrounging a lot of bits and pieces. Since I was so busy during the week with the range practice, and the important consideration regarding the choice of what branch of the service I would choose, plus of course, the attention I was giving Ann, I completely overlooked the fact that I was to forward my mother the one pound postal order and my request for her to contact her money lending friend in Dublin for the loan for me to purchase a new wardrobe. So how much cash did I require? I heard that there was a fifty shilling Tailoring Company shop up in Patrick Street, Cork, and that all suits for that price were ready made, but were only suitable for farmers and hillbillies. That avenue was therefore, definitely closed. Then, I learned that Burtons, also in Patrick Street, were reasonably alright, if you don't buy off the rail, instead go for a made-to-measure outfit, but that would take some time, and the cost was estimated at approximately thirteen pounds for a suit and overcoat. In the meantime I was without civvies of any kind, so I immediately headed back up to the wooden nissan huts, then situated between the Martello Tower and the handball alley, where the signal's division were housed to discuss a deal with the Blusher concerning another loan of his suit and overcoat. But when he insisted on another ten shillings for their use I refused and instead, offered him seven pounds cash for them both, when I received my money from my mother the following week. He readily agreed because he was due to be transferred to a ship, and he felt they would have been destroyed by the dirty conditions on board. I then handed him a ten shilling note as a deposit, and he allowed me to remove them to my quarters, where I immediately let down the turnups on the trousers and then pressed every part of the suit and overcoat and hung them both in my locker.

Later that evening, when a group of us had returned to the billet and while we were listening to Nat King Cole, Dean Martin, Eddie Fisher, and others on the radio, the subject turned to the branch of the service which we had decided on, and Paddy McCormack said that he heard that there were two real gobshites in the mechanical training bay, a certain chief engine room artificer they called the "Geef" and an individual who had absolutely no qualifications except that he knew the most senior officer in the service. McCormack also added that they had no modern equipment down there for training anybody.

I didn't believe a word of it, so I simply turned my attention to the radio again (Pye Model P74, as I recall), while Rosemary Clooney was singing *Hey There, You, with the Stars in Your Eyes*, and I started thinking about Ann ashore in Cobh, and what might she be doing right now. After breakfast the next day it was back to the same routine once more, of billet cleaning. The well mannered PO Louie McKiernan was the NCO in charge of the unit, and without any bullying or ordering us about, the work was undertaken under his guidance in a very short time indeed, and my responsibility this time was to ensure that all beds were made up in the regulation military fashion. When that task was completed, I was free to return to the civvy canteen, where I met the usual visitors, who were speaking to crew members of the Maev, one of our three ships. I overheard them speaking about Smerwick Harbour, Clew Bay, the Bull Rock, the Blaskets, the Saltees, and Scotsman's Bay, and I wondered quietly to myself for I was too shy to ask, were they foreign ports, because that last name certainly seemed to be so, and as I listened they all spoke of contempt towards the ships (as if they truly hated them); of the terrible seas that they had encountered on their return to base, and of the horrible dirty and degrading conditions on board. I also remembered something Stretch told me earlier about the ships' crews, they did indeed smell and look very dirty.

On my return to the base I visited Nan Coveney in the post office and purchased a two pound postal order and a stamp for the envelope, and enclosed a short note explaining to my mother that I required seven pounds without delay from her Jew man friend. As I approached the naval pier on the way back to our rooms, I met Kerry Byrnes who explained to me that Sergeant Ned Curtis then the person in charge of the military police and the most hated and feared man ever in Haulbowline had Gene O'Shea the man who introduced himself to me on my arrival as the Guard

Commander, under close military arrest, and was escorting him to their compound for interrogation, concerning the disappearance of several pounds of butter, three pounds of tea, and eight pounds of beef missing from the supply stores. A witness stated that he saw O'Shea wrapping up the food carefully in grease proof paper, and then hiding the goods amongst the swill which he collected around the various cookhouses to feed his pigs ashore. Byrnes further explained that acting on that information, Curtis and his staff searched through the pig feeding on the boat that was heading for Cobh, and found the stolen goods in barrels, but the cute Kerryman rightly refused to make a statement and the witness was warned off by a friend of Genes, a Senior NCO living on the island, and therefore, the case was dropped due to insufficient evidence. That food was returned to the stores and was promptly brought ashore the following evening by an assistant for his own personal consumption. I shall return to the infamous Ned Curtis in due course.

After mass the following Sunday, I decided that once and for all, I would somehow bring up the subject of foreign trips in the billet, once the subject of ships is mentioned by anyone. Sure enough, my chance came when Spud Murphy said he met Jim Roche, who was a crew member of the Maev, ashore. Then, I immediately said, without thinking, "Did he say anything about voyages to foreign ports?" "Are you fucking serious?" Bully White said, "They are never sent anywhere, because they are afraid they would break down and have to be towed back by a civvy tug and really be disgraced". Peachie Hume then shouted over from the window, "Don't you know any fucking thing, Brady? The last time they left the coastline was in 1954, when they went to Stockholm and Antwerp, and I bet you, they will never go anywhere, because not only are they afraid they will break down, the are terrified they will spring a large leak and sink with all hands". I suspected that this was just crap talk, and with the lawyer now moved to take up an appointment as an Officers' Waiter, no less, I had no way of verifying that information.

So I shall have to wait and see for myself when I am posted out to join one of the vessels. Firstly, I have to be technically trained and instructed. As far as I was concerned, I was about to become a highly skilled professional in my chosen branch of the service before I was to be allowed near the ships, and the next morning, I was to report to the mechanical training bay immediately after parade. When that great moment came, Tony Lee was assigned to escort me down and introduce me to the staff and to explain the type of machinery, machine parts, and engines that were available to work and train on, and also the classroom, and the various precision tools that would also be of particular use to me whenever I was dispatched to sea. As we walked the short distance to the mechanical training bay, which was until then out of bounds to me, I was full of excitement, for here was I, an uneducated boy from Ballyfermot, about to become a technician at the taxpayers expense, but only after I had suffered the extreme hardship of the Recruits' Division along with its threats, bullying, and bollocking. I now felt that this big break to finally achieve a skilled trade through working with the latest machinery was only what I worked for, and deserved. Then as Tony lifted the catch of the green coloured wooden wicket door marked M T Bay, I thought "if only my mother could see me now", and immediately on entering, L S Tighe Kane said, "You are just in time for tea, before we start anything. When that's over, you can sweep the floor and carry in more coal for that pot bellied stove".

Well, at least, I was assigned to some useful employment, right from the beginning. But I wondered "Where's the heavy or even light machinery required for my grasp of the knowledge that's required for this profession?" Then, while we were sipping our mugs of tar-like tea, which had been boiled on the steel stove, I decided to look around this whitewashed shed type building, which was obviously once a boat house, for its rear door was connected to a slipway leading down to the sea. To my left, was a wooden bench, the length of the room, and firmly bolted into place were a few vices, and a couple of hacksaws lying around, mixed with a number of small tools suitable for repairing lawn-mowers, a dismantled tiny lawn-mowers' petrol engine, a seven pound sledge hammer, some oily rags and one small oil can. To my right was a belt driven lathe, drill and grindstone, all supplied with a small portion of wood placed under them to stand on while working at them. Also in position was a large heavy duty engineering drill, and according to Tighe Kane who appeared elderly to me only the lathe and grindstone actually worked, and that only the tradesmen called engine room artificers were allowed to use them. "And how" I asked, "could I become a tradesman?" "Well, son", he replied, with a little sadness in his voice, "first you have to have the Intermediate Certificate from school; then you could apply for a position in the army apprentice school in Naas, and then if you are accepted through an interview and on your school's record (I was without one), it's several years hard studying in their well equipped workshop, with stiff exams every year and a very difficult one the final year before you are classed as an ERA". "But what am I to become down here?" Tighe like a father figure, continued. "Well, to be perfectly honest, when you complete your time here, you will be an ordinary stoker, similar to a one star private in the army. Then as you progress, you should eventually become an AB, or a three star private, a fully trained individual. Then, with a few good breaks, excellent conduct, and above all, hard work, it's possible to end up like me, a leading Stoker, which is equivalent to a Corporal in the army".

I was definitely impressed, so I asked Padge Farrelly to show me around this whitewashed shed they were all insisting on calling a "training bay", which was packed with ancient machinery with all their brass fittings almost polished away, and the remainder of them painted with battleship grey paint scrounged from one of the ships. Behind the building, and lying in a corner was a disused forge, clearly untouched for many years, perhaps since the British abandoned this place, and a few foam fire extinguishers were lying around after being discharged, possibly during a demonstration. As we continued our tour I was introduced to a pair of perfect gentlemen who were in one way or another to have a very positive bearing on my future, CPO Rory McCarthy, whom I mentioned earlier as the church singer, and PO Johnny O'Brien, who immediately volunteered to complete the conducted tour. Further to the rear, was a miniature boiler of the type fitted on the corvettes; a scotch fire tube marine type boiler, which was used as a training vehicle for students such as myself. But in fact it was only a slightly larger type than those which are installed for domestic heating, and were of no significant importance when it came to the operating of the genuine boilers on the ships, which between the pair of them, almost occupied a quarter of the entire ship's size. However, PO O'Brien continued up to the upstairs section of the building, entered by a half rotten steel staircase until we reached a plywood partitioned room with an uncovered wooden floor similar to the billets, and the only fitting in this thirty foot long room was the outline of the ship's water and fuel pumping system and mind you no ship's model of any sort, and no mention of what class of ships we possessed, their tonnage, what guns they carried, or what anti-submarine weapons were fitted to them. The only other item worth mentioning was the classroom, which had several desks, a blackboard, and its floor was covered in heavy duty brown lino. To the left of the classroom was what they referred to as the "Electrician's Training Bay", and as I glanced through the dividing door I could clearly observe that at least they were in possession of a bank of heavy duty vehicle batteries which were on charge, and an electrically operated buffer for touching up brass wear. The excellent NCO then in command of that unit was CPO P J Crowe.

It was rapidly appearing to me that I was serving in an outfit that was clearly pretending to be a naval service with three second world war ships, that I hadn't yet served on, but were obviously unreliable and possible a danger to sail on. They were also criminally ill-equipped, and the entire business would be laughable were it not so bloody serious. We operated on strict Royal Navy codes and traditions at sea and ashore, and yet the only really trained Royal Naval officer was the Director of the Service, a certain H Jerome. So to be perfectly honest I was beginning to feel sorry for the entire show, particularly those who were really trying, but they weren't helped by a particular officer in the office, and Ferriter down in recruits both of whom were former junior personnel who only attained promotion, when they entered the young naval service after the war. Even at this stage, I was positive that I would not gain much experience down in this shed, so I would have to wait until my posting came through, and that was not to be for several months, according to the officer in charge who ordered me to his hut that he called an office. "Brady", he started, "my policy is to weed out loafers and dodgers who don't fit in to this division, and if you don't come up to scratch, you're out and into the seaman's department. Is that perfectly clear?" "Yes". "Yes, Sir, you address me, and stand to attention when you speak to an officer. Now. go back down below and report to the CPO. It was apparent that myself and that officer were never to get along together. The "Geef" his assistant, could also be nasty when it suited him. Although he was undoubtedly qualified as an engine room tradesman, he did on many occasions arrange to have certain personnel who he had disliked transferred to the ships as replacements, even though that person or persons would not have been due for posting for perhaps six months, or even a year. On one particular occasion, that vicious action was enacted because a certain PO, only one rank below himself refused to run an errand to purchase a packet of cigarettes for the Geef. Nasty and uncaring individuals are in all walks of life, but in a military disciplined establishment, on a tiny island, like Haulbowline, where several hundred men of all ages are grouped together, life can be extremely trying. Anyway, the Geef took the damn place too bloody seriously, and really imagined that the building was in fact a fully-equipped and fitted workshop, when in reality almost all his working life was occupied within that structure repairing lawnmowers which were in the care of another extreme oddity, the infamous CPO Batt Sullivan.

Before I continue, just a few words about the Batt. It was agreed by all that he was a rogue and a liar, and there were thousands of stories around about him. Some were true, and most were false, but what was undoubtedly true was that he was in America in the 1920s and produced photographs to prove that. It was also clear that he was involved with the criminal mobs over there, but his confessed association with Al Capone were never proved. What was common knowledge was that he was deported from the States as an undesirable, and that soon afterwards, he enlisted in the Marine Service (the Naval Service's predecessor), where he rose fairly quickly through the ranks to become a very questionable CPO for he never really acted or looked the part of a senior NCO and never gained the respect due to that rank. He is another individual I shall return to later on.

Meanwhile, the show goes on down in the M T Bay, where Tighe made the tar-like tea every hour, and since the department was short staffed, Brady is detailed as the floor sweeper, to brasso the idle machinery and door handles, and as the messenger, in fact, the general dogs body. But, it must be remembered that then I was the lowest form of life. To make matters worse I was also ordered to help Ingo down in the dining hall as his assistant for a few weeks. This unwelcome duty is an extra responsibility added to your normal routine, which of course means extra hours, because the dining hall attendants are never finished until approximately two hours after meal times. Ingo obviously had everything under firm control after a long period in that employment and thankfully, that included some of the cooks, and he also enjoyed easy access to the main cookhouses and their storeroom, which was to become extremely useful for the immediate future. After some time slaving in that place, I noticed that during the cooking of the meals for all the ratings, the duty cook, plus the PO in charge of cooks, while he was present, would stir the huge containers of tea, which would be boiling on the stove, with the wooden handle of the nearest sweeping brush, while adding the meat browning liquid from a bottle, which as I stated earlier, was to give the tea the impression that it was strong with plenty of tea added, when in fact, it was little more than hot coloured water. Nobody paid any attention to this illegal behaviour until the Annual General Headquarters Inspection was in progress, and when the army colonels visited the cookhouse, everyone including Ingo, and myself and the entire cooking staff were attired in their white starched uniforms, with the best pots and pans, and delph displayed in the best possible position. However, the overall cookhouse boss forgetting the important occasion, continued throughout the close inspection to stir the container of tea with a brush handle which had been resting beside a senior Colonel, and added the correct dosage of browning to the beverage. The unwelcome army's top brass were outraged and on their immediate return to Dublin presented a damning report to the Chief of Staff and poor PO Paddy Kennedy was offered a dreadful choice: resign or volunteer to join a ship. He chose the posting on the ship, but since he was almost three times our average ages, and regarded by us as elderly, he therefore was to suffer for his sins on the Maev, where I was to sail with him in due course.

First Trip to Cork

The weeks were now flying by since I had escaped from recruit training, and the film, 'The Cruel Sea' was finishing its long run in the Savoy in Cork the coming weekend. Therefore, I phoned Ann in Fords and explained to her that I had been presented with two tickets, which had to be used by that Saturday, and would she accompany me up to Cork early that afternoon, and that after the picture we could enjoy a nice meal in their restaurant, and then go across to Mooney's Lounge, before we travelled back on the twenty past eleven train. I had checked everything out concerning 'The Cruel Sea' just to impress her. I found out from friends that the film was made in 1953 and that Jack Hawkins was cast as the captain, and Stanley Baker as the first officer. It was written by Eric Amber and directed by Charles Frend. The also informed me that what was missing was the sea sickness and the stinking smell. That was to reach me later. In the meantime, Ann was excited at the prospect of a day out, and she promised she would meet me in Cobh station, wearing something nice, and I added "Use lots of that sexy perfume that you usually wear". "OK", she whispered over the phone, and all was settled.

When Saturday eventually come around again, my thoughts were firmly on that stunning girl in Cobh, and as I prepared myself to proceed ashore, there was a heated argument taking place in the washhouse between rival groups of soccer supporters, of a Cork team and the local heroes Cobh Ramblers, and for the first time since I enlisted I feared for the life of someone, and to this day I will never forget the hate that was directed to that fanatical ramblers supporter, Billy Brannigan. That savage row and others that I have since encountered, have taught me to never argue about religion, politics, or any form of football for it invariably leads to the loss of friendships forever. Even as the John Wyndham made its way across to Cobh, the argument between Brannigan continued, and I interrupted them by saying "It's not worth it lads, it's only a game, with growing men running after a ball". That mouthful only gave them temporary food for thought, and then the ridiculous debate continued.

Thankfully, Ann was waiting at the station when I arrived, and since the train had not yet reached the station from Cork, we decided to wait in the tea rooms, where we ordered a pot of tea and sandwiches, and although the tea's quality was similar to that which I was served in Cork on my first journey, I then discovered for the first time, that one's company in particular situations can make a vast difference for the tea on this occasion tasted better, even though it looked the same, and indeed it was the same as before. We boarded the train without delay, when it entered the station, and I was struck by the number of carriages the engine was pulling, and by the amount of shopping the

Another whitewashed shed. Recruits training on the Pom-Pom gun in 1955.

The army top brass during inspection.

"Actions Stations" Pom-Pom gun crew in action off the South Coast.

Firing the 20 M.M. Oerlikon anti aircraft gun during exercises off the South Coast.

Leaving Dublin at 9.00 a.m. aboard the Maev in the 1950's.

L.E. Maev's 4 inch gun.

Forced to dig trenches at gunpoint! Glen of Imaal 1959. Stretch on left, Author centre, Peter Malone right.

"Doyler" photograph taken by Author.

Author (centre row left), Stretch (centre same row), Doyler on his left.

The C.O. Cmdr. Petie Kavanagh greeted aboard H.M.S. Tyne in Cork Harbour by the British commander-in-Chief home fleet in January 1961.

C.P.O. "Paddles" McKeown coxswain of the Cliona in 1963.

L.E. Grainne.

L.E. Banba.

L.E. Fola.

L.E. Deirdre under construction, Cork Verolme Dockyard 1971.

L.E. Deirdre, on sea trials shortly after her launching.

train's full compliment of passengers were carrying. Indeed on its return journey to Cobh almost all compartments were fully occupied. Those days were long before the motor car became so widely used. However, when Ann and I reached Cork's station, we headed straight to the Savoy for the early showing of the highly recommended 'The Cruel Sea', which I knew was to run for 126 minutes, and just as we sat in our seats, I was very surprised and happy when a very large organ appeared, it seemed, from below the stage, and a gentleman immediately commenced playing popular tunes such as Mario Lanza's *Drinking Song*, and *I'll Walk with God*; Doris Day's, *Secret Love*; Frank Chacksfield's *Limelight*; Guy Mitchell's *There's a Pawnshop on a Corner in Pittsburgh, Pennsylvania*, and amongst many others, Perry Como's big hit, *Don't Let the Stars Get in Your Eyes*, and before very long, the entire congregation was singing along, obviously delighted in perfect harmony. Then I turned to Ann and said, "Isn't this marvellous entertainment? You pay at the door to view a movie and a magnificent side show such as this is provided free of charge". It can be stated that I was well and truly hyped up in advance of this film. I even heard that when it reached Dublin, the entire crew of one of our ships, which was tied up alongside the quays, were marched up to the Adelphi Cinema in Middle Abbey Street to view it at the State's expense.

So, it was therefore obvious that I couldn't wait until it started, and I was so preoccupied with the expectations of the film that even as Ann spoke to me I was unable to hear her. When it finally commenced I became even more engrossed, for I imagined myself in Jack Hawkins' position, as Commander of the 'Compass Rose', sinking more U-Boats than any other captain in the Royal Navy, and winning the battle of the Atlantic, almost single-handedly, and when I saw the beautiful lines of the Corvette, used in the movie, I wondered why our Government had refused the loan of one of our ships which they had purchased from the British to star in the film. However, my comrades were correct, the smell of the ship and the seasickness were missing. In later viewings I found it vastly overrated as a war movie, because on close inspection, many of the scenes were clearly shot in studio water tanks. When the screening was completed, I as promised, escorted Ann down to the Savoy's magnificent restaurant which occupied almost an entire floor, and treated herself and myself to a mixed grill, before strolling over to Mooneys for a couple of drinks, and then rush up for the train journey home. On the way back the carriages were again full to capacity, and as we walked towards her home she told me how much she enjoyed her evening out, and that the next time we visit Cork it would be her treating me with a visit to the Cork Opera House. "Opera" I said, "What's that?" As she began to explain the five minute warning sign of our last launch sounded and I hurried back to catch it.

The Scams

The remainder of the weekend passed without anything out of the ordinary happening, which is unusual within an area of less than thirty acres which is occupied by several hundred personnel at any given time. So, it will be appreciated that with that number of very young and very fit men function on such a small section of an island with very little recreational or other facilities available, their excess energy must be released somehow, and naturally because I cannot be everywhere at once or hear about everything that takes place, I am only relating some of the events that actually happened. However, by chance, my position as mess man, (or its common term, "dish washer"), in the dining hall with Ingo proved to be a marvellous venue for overhearing gossip. While clearing off the tables and washing the dishes, I picked up juicy morsels, for instance, about the officers' behaviour up in their mess. One evening while Smudger was forcing down a feed of shepherds pie with his cronies, he revealed a handful of real good secrets. Firstly, he explained that he was the barman in the mess and that like any barman in any pub, he always sees his customers in their worst possible condition, and in that state they talk through their arses, and sometimes act like pigs. He continued to name officers' wives who were having affairs with other officers' husbands, while certain officers were at sea and on courses. How one Lt-Cmdr was having a serious relationship with the wife of a rating who lived in the base's married quarters, how he showed her off in the officers' mess, and that by listening to their conversations, he knew where they met and where they stayed in Dublin and in other localities ashore, plus the variety of flowers and other presents that he presented her with. He then related to a very interested and attentive audience, how the officers behaved amongst themselves while they were away from the rank and file, and how many of them reacted violently and otherwise after the consumption of excess alcohol. According to Smudger, one senior officer was observed on his hands and knees crawling around the mess floor barking like a dog with drink dribbling from his mouth. Then, as Ingo overheard this enlightening revelation, he added that one of the captains on a ship entertained the crew when he was drunk, by tap dancing on their mess tables while playing a mouth organ, and that he also assembled the ship's crew ashore in Killybegs to attack and beat up a group of civvies, because they had insulted him in a public bar earlier in the evening. He then added that the same commissioned officer and gentleman was barred from the pub down beside the gasometer on the Dublin quays, because he abused the owner again while he was twisted drunk. Smudger then interrupted Ingo and said "Listen you lot, do you want to hear something really great?" Nobody answered and then he dropped the bombshell, and disclosed how a fantastic fiddle was operated. In those days a credit book was operated from the mess whereby the officers order drink, cigarettes, or food; sign for it, and then pay the bill when they received their cheques at the end of the month. The waiters and the barmen then discovered that none of the officers ever questioned the amount that was payable, nor the range of goods that they had signed for. Consequently, their little brains began working overtime, and within a very short period of time the entire staff who belonged to the mess, were able to copy every officer's signature. When a particular officer socialised with his friends, several rounds would be ordered, and the amount taken would not be recalled, so he simply signed the credit book not knowing for exactly what. Alternatively, the waiter simply signed the officer's name himself for something he would never see, for instance twenty 'Churchman', or 'Craven A' cigarettes, and pocket them for his own pleasure. One officer in particular, 'Snags', suspected that something peculiar was happening, and consequently insisted that no empty glasses be removed from his table while he was drinking, thereby ensuring that by the end of the evening he was aware of how many drinks he had consumed, and only signed for that amount.

Haulbowline was a university of life where no qualifications were required for entry, and I was learning fast and enjoying that free tuition. But not down in the mechanical training bay, or the "technical training bay", as some called it. Why I really don't know, because as I explained earlier, there was nothing technical stored, fitted or operating there, and their important sounding titles meant absolutely nothing. For months I was taught damn all, except how to start up the stove for tea, collect broken down lawnmowers from the Batt, clean out the swimming pool on occasions, and how to operate the foam fire extinguishers that were used for putting out oil fires. This boring repetition was strangling me, so I asked the Geef for an interview to see the divisional officer to request him to post me to a ship without delay. He replied that I was needed where I was, and when I asked, "doing what?", he simply ordered me to stand to attention and not to speak to an officer without being spoken to. A very nasty piece of work was our officer in charge, and that was agreed by many of those who were unfortunate to come in contact with him.

You may recall that, at the beginning of this narrative I mentioned that almost everyone down in the base was tagged with a nickname, including myself. So therefore, it's only proper that I explain how I acquired mine. One evening while working late with Ingo in the dining hall, he announced that he had a solid date with another girl named Ann in Carragaloe, and could I hurry, since he wanted to catch the ten past eight boat out, because according to him, she had faithfully promised him the lot for free. I, of course, readily agreed, for who am I to obstruct two young lovers? So, at once, I gathered at least twenty-five side plates and headed to the sink, where Ingo was waiting to receive them, when suddenly, I skidded on a discarded rasher and landed flat on my back, with all the delph smashed around me. A moment later Lt Chippy Carney the duty officer entered the building during his rounds, and asked what was causing all the commotion. Ingo replied "Sir, that fucking eejit, Brady, has mashed all our plates". "Well, Brady", the officer continued, "you'll have to pay barrack damages and it will be deducted from your wages". "But, Sir", I pleaded, "I'm hardly getting anything as it is!" He simply ignored me and continued on his tour. From that moment on, I was and still continue to be referred to as "The Masher" Brady. Some even become confused, and imagine that I was in a serious brawl and mashed my opponent; others, especially girls, on hearing my name, consulted a dictionary, and concluded that I was a ladies' man! Oddly, when anyone down there was presented with a nickname, it stuck very rapidly, and their christian names (which were, I'm sure, considered very carefully by their parents before it was finally selected for them), was automatically discarded for a name they thought more appropriate for them.

Several evenings later, with nothing better to do, I visited the billet, where the potential NCOs were housed. As I entered, I noticed that everybody was extremely quiet, except for a boxing commentator, who was describing a big fight that had taken place in America, possibly between Archie Moore and Floyd Patterson. Listening were two terrific naval boxers, who were unbeaten, Gay Callaghan and Dermo Deeney, and as the night wore on, Cider arrived from the wet canteen along with Muxer, Pinhead, Doyler, and the Pidgeon, and between them, they were carrying six flagons of Bulmers, and four large bottles of Guinness, all on tick, according to them. However, when the drink was consumed, Callaghan and Muxer decided that we needed something to soak up the gargle. Because the canteen was closed since before eleven, and since the main food store and cookhouse were both locked and impregnable, the NCO mess was the most vulnerable, where food would be available. So armed with only a large screwdriver and a pinchers, they entered the back window, and after a long struggle, they removed the door of the fridge. They then removed four large sides of fresh salmon, belonging to the poacher "Mugu" and fried the lot undetected on the coal burning fire, which was still burning since teatime. It was my first taste of any salmon, never mind wild salmon, poached from the River Lee the night before by Mugu and another professional poacher, a young seaman. Mugu was a torpedo and depth charge expert, having been fully trained during years of experience in the Royal Navy, before joining our outfit. He was, of course, highly respected within the service, and he was also the highest ranking NCO living on the island, over the NCOs mess. Anyway, after every scrap of fish was removed from the bones, we gathered all the skin and bones, and wrapped everything very carefully into a sheet of brown paper and tied them up with a piece of twine, and then Muxer volunteered to place the parcel outside the hall door of Sgt Ned Curtis the head policeman, who also lived on the island. Of course, the following morning, half of the base's establishment was ordered for questioning by Curtis and his staff in the policeman's building, but thankfully, nobody talked and the case was never solved. I also mentioned here before that Curtis was the most hated man ever in Haulbowline, not just because he was dressed in that green army uniform with the red cap bands, but because of Curtis's approach to his job. The others followed his style of going after everyone, just for the sake of it, and making life very difficult.

They spied on us around the base, in the living quarters, around the cookhouses, in the messes, and one was placed on the boats to search us as we went ashore to meet our girlfriends and others. Curtis used to make it a point to get out of his bed early each morning and leave his wife and children to meet the first boat in from Cobh, which carried the day's supply of bread and milk, because he was convinced that someone was devouring huge amounts of it during the short voyage across. From a hilltop overlooking the naval pier, he sat, binoculars in hand, for weeks during the summer, for hard evidence, so as to secure a conviction. What he didn't know was that in fact much of the missing food was divided and handed out before the boat actually left its berth at Cobh, and it was then taken away by several servicemen to help nourish their large families. Curtis did eventually catch an unsuspecting new recruit, alongside Haulbowline, drinking a jam jar of ice cold milk from a churn. He charged him and marched the recruit before the CO. When Tommy McKenna asked him why he stole the milk, he quietly said "Sir, it was because I was starving". "That's no excuse", replied McKenna, "you get adequate food in your rations, so I am finding you five shillings, and the next time you are caught stealing other people's rations, I will send you to the Military Prison (The Digger)". Curtis was delighted with that result and that night down in the NCO's mess, he was overheard boasting to his assistants how he had solved the food stealing case single-handedly. In fact, two POs who were listening nearby, were part of the ring who were removing the food from the supply boat over in Cobh.

I will relate one more incident involving the head policeman, before I continue. A very attractive and very expensive piano was discovered in a disused office by a PO. Apparently the desirable instrument had been stored away, and then forgotten about. However, after viewing and measuring the find, he decided that it would fit perfectly into his living room ashore, as well as helping to educate his children, entertaining his guests, for his wife could manage a few tunes. It would, apart from all that, impress all those who would visit his modest home in Cobh. But first, how was it to be smuggled ashore under the eagle eyes of the dreaded red caps? He waited until finally his moment arrived, when stage props were required for a play being performed ashore, and to which Curtis was to be attending. On the afternoon of the first night's performance, all the props that were being used were assembled in the drillshed, and then the piano was simply added to the collection, and when the equipment arrived in Cobh, it was loaded onto the van for delivery and a slight detour was made to unload the precious cargo, before the remainder was brought to the theatre. Incidentally, an antique rifle found in a store room was smuggled across on that same day, hidden between two pieces of old timber. Where there's a will, there's a way!

Anyway, it was Saturday again, and time to start preparing for shore leave to see my divine redhead. So it was back to the washhouse for yet another wash and maybe a shave if there was anything to shave. Believe it or not, the same gang were attempting to sing, and they were not really bad, for I believe that it was the echo that was generated in the room which was responsible for that illusion. Paddy Smith had a fairly good crooner's voice, and he was passable , imitating Bing Crosby, and he also made a good job of *Answer Me*, by Nat King Cole. Jack Banim and Georgie Long were again trying the very popular *Three Coins in the Fountain*. When you hear them all singing or attempting to sing, you may be positive that they have a certain date ashore. But there were a large number of others who preferred the company of their mates as drinking partners. Anyway, I got ready as quickly as possible, and along with my now close friends, Stretch and Doyler, we caught the ten past seven boat again, and on this trip we were ferried across by the boat which was normally used for carrying cargo, because at the last moment, she was pressed into service. Well, it was all the same to us, we only wanted to reach the women by whatever means possible. Anyway, when we arrived down in the Well House, everyone present was in a sombre mood, for Andy was again away in hospital, and some relation of his was running the place, and charging the full price, and I actually heard

Bobby Hume complaining that he was charged two shillings and nine pence for twenty 'Sweet Afton' cigarettes.

Shortly before eight, I again left to meet Ann, down outside the Commodore. This time I was positive she would turn up, well she did eventually, at eight fifteen. But she explained to me "It's a woman's privilege to be late, and it goes to prove that you don't take women for granted". However, I didn't argue because I would have waited all night for the privilege of her charming company. On the way down to the pictures again, we only had time for one drink, and as we both sat down that mouth Muxer, who by now had a good few drinks taken, shouted across to her and said to watch me because I was only a dirty fucker who only wanted one thing from a woman, and that was sex. "Is that true Jim?", she asked, with a very worried and puzzled look on her face. "No, Ann", I replied, "can't you see he is only a drunkard who is jealous of me in your company?" "Now, Jim", she continued, with a determined look on her face, "if you have a bad reputation over here with girls, I'll drop you like a hot potato, and don't you forget it". "No, Ann I won't", I answered softly, and I swore to myself that I would get that bastard Muxer for trying to fuck things up for me. We then headed directly down to the Ormonde, or as the locals called it, the Tower Cinema, and again, as we arrived, only then did we discover that the movie showing was another classic, 'Casablanca', starring Humphrey Bogard and Ingrid Bergman. Although I have seen it perhaps ten times since, it still reminds me of that night with the redhead. Anyway, before the film commenced, the cinema operations again played the classical music, and my partner again could easily identify the composers. She named Beethoven, Mozart, Brahms, and they repeated the playing of Tchaikovsky's *Nutcracker Suite*, which I remembered they had played the first time we had visited this place. During the screening of the film, and again when we left she asked me over and over again, if it was true what the foul-mouthed Muxer had said about me down in the bar. "No", I replied as gently as I could,

"You Ann are the first girl I ever met". "I wish I could believe you, Jim", she said, as tears were entering her eyes. "because to kiss a girl so tenderly as you do, takes a lot of experience. But don't you ever let me down, or that would be the end of our relationship forever". "No, Ann, I promise. Then all is settled?" "Yes", she replied. As we approached her hall door, I held her neck with both hands and held her firmly towards me, then gently kissed her on both ears and on her soft lips. I promised that I would phone her at work as soon as possible and she again reminded me that the next journey to Cork was her treat to me, and that we would be visiting the Opera House. My instant reply was "We're not going to see Opera, whatever that is". But she said, "they stage plays there, and musicals". This, I concluded was becoming far too confusing for a youngster from a large corporation complex, so I simply said, "OK I'm heading back to the boat because it's nearly five past twelve". So I hurried down the hill and as before, I jumped aboard the John Adams, as she was departing from The Department of Defence pier.

A long uninteresting period when nothing out of the ordinary happened, was suddenly transformed when a pregnant mother was unable to travel ashore for medical assistance, and medical attention was unable to reach her due to a storm, since all passenger boats were tied up alongside the piers. The wife of a serviceman living in the married quarters only managed to reach the guardroom where a healthy baby was delivered with the assistance of the Doc and another lady from the island undertaking the duties of a midwife. During that same severe storm, a very large galvanised steel roof was whipped off an old building at the back of the island, which struck CPO Tom Guilfoyle, killing him instantly. His companion's life, however, was saved by faith, for only a moment earlier, Dave Cronin had been called back aboard the *Maev* by Hal Halligan to post a letter.

Some weeks after the above events, my low opinion of Ferriter was vindicated for when all available personnel were assembled for the Commanding Officer's inspection, he announced to everybody present, including all the senior and junior officers, that from then on he would, without exception to anyone, be addressed as "Sir" because he had just been promoted to the new rank of senior Chief Petty Officer. He then proceeded to demonstrate the proper method of wiping one's behind with a piece of toilet paper, thankfully without removing his trousers, for that, I am positive, would have frightened the life out of all the young men present. Obviously, after that half-witted demonstration his standing, though always low, was completely destroyed. It appears that the civil servants were bitterly complaining about the high usage of toilet paper, which was, and still is, useless for its intended purpose, because it's similar to grease proof paper, and without going into too much detail, it's clearly obvious that because of its smoothness, much more paper is used to perform its delicate task. Ferriter then personally decided that he should explain to all, how to minimise its usage. Because of this pathetic behaviour on the square, and his demand that he (although still only an NCO) should be addressed as "Sir", made him the laughing stock of the establishment for very many months and it was remarked by many that he should have stayed in the army as a corporal.

After the above welcome break from the normal routine, the mundane life returned with a vengeance, and it was murdering me, so it was therefore clear, that I was quite unsuitable to ever becoming a serviceman for life. The army had been brought back from the dead when it was agreed by the government that our forces would participate in United Nations peacekeeping operations abroad, and even today the troops are lining up to volunteer for overseas duties which provides them with the opportunities to travel the world and undertake real soldiering instead of sitting around in crumbling barrack rooms, year after year doing nothing, and serving no useful purpose whatsoever. So with that in mind I again approached my divisional officer and requested to be transferred to one of the vessels. On this occasion, he wasn't too nasty and therefore, simply replied that in a couple of months, Halligan and Roche would be returning to base, and Tierney and myself would be replacing them on the Maev. In the meantime, I was still not learning anything worthwhile down in the M T Bay, because as I already explained there were no machines that worked, and no parts of corvettes engine room or boiler room there to teach me about how anything aboard ship operated. Therefore, I would have to wait until I arrived on the ship, and then learn the job by trial and error, mostly error, I suspected.

A Journey in Style

In the meantime, I was lucky to have Ann ashore to visit, which, apart from anything else, greatly helped to relieve the boredom, but unfortunately, I was only in a position to see her occasionally in the immediate future, since I was now repaying the loan which my mother secured for me to purchase the suit and overcoat. A couple of guard duties were also on the horizon. After that, I would be entitled to a short period of leave, plus a travelling warrant to my home address in Dublin, and I intended making that journey in style, dressed in my No 1 uniform, to impress my mother, and the neighbours, and anyone else who I might encounter. But first comes the guard room responsibilities. From all reports which I had assembled from various sources around the base, it was apparent that to undertake the guardroom obligations was not a cushy number. Firstly, you had to change into your No 2 uniform, complete with a whitened canvas belt and leggings, along with the heavy hob nailed boots, and would you believe, a second world war tin hat, painted army green, which resembled a deep soup plate. Secondly, you fall in, outside the guardroom at six in the evening and then remain on duty until you are relieved by the day shift the following morning at eight. Now comes the hardest part! That fourteen hour's continuous obligation commences after you have completed your normal day's work, and during that period, you were ordered out of your beds at 6am, during the summer, and 7am in the winter. So it was clear that by the time the guard was mounted and inspected by the officer of the day the entire crew was already tired, and then deserved a well earned rest.

Therefore, when my name appeared on the main notice board along with Redmond and Deniffe plus Dinny Horgan as Commander, I decided to take to the bunk earlier the night before in order to gain some extra sleep. I turned in at nine that evening, and just as I was beginning to drift away, the usual gang, including Mynes, Muxer Cider, Hector, and the rest marched in to the billet singing their heads off, and again loaded up with bottles of Bulmers and Guinness, for another party that lasted until after 1am. The following day I was obviously knackered and I was certain that I would never last through the night without falling asleep on my feet. Shortly after Lt Sullivan inspected us, Dinny Horgan ordered me down to the cookhouse to collect the guardroom rations. Luckily, my townie, Larry was the duty cook, and instead of the normal quota, I returned with a stone of potatoes, about three pounds of butter cut from a fifty six pound slab, around two pounds of streaky rashers and approximately the same weight of fat sausages. That lot reminded me of the amount of food that was present in the same premises that faithful first night that I had arrived down in Haulbowline.

When the last boat in from Cobh was tied up for the night, and when all the base's personnel were secured in their quarters, it was time to build up our solid fuel fire and prepare the frying pan for our feast. Redmond had some experience of cooking, so he was the obvious choice as the chef of the night, with me as his assistant, cutting bread, peeling the potatoes, which were also to be fried, drawing coal from the bunker, and washing and then heating the plates for the three of us. At this stage, Deniffe was outside on guard, watching out for the duty officer, rather than guarding the base and everything was eventually fried. The total was divided in three and then I delivered Deniffe's share outside to where he was posted as lookout, along with six slices of white pan bread and a mug of strong tea to help keep him awake. We then switched on the old Philip's Radio and tuned into AFN, the American Forces Station, operating somewhere in Europe, possibly West Germany. At that time of night, we could receive various European Stations very clearly indeed, and on this occasion, we were listening to Frank Sinatra singing *Young at Heart*, and *Love and Marriage*; Frankie Laine singing *High Noon*; and the Platters, *Only You*. All the above were huge smash hits of that period.

When I finished eating I was bursting with food, and then Dinny directed me to relieve Deniffe for the following hour, which I was thankful for, because I was beginning to feel sleepy inside sitting at the warm fire after devouring so much welcome food. Outside the night was perfectly still with absolutely no wind and the only sounds were the soft tone of the base clock ringing out the time every fifteen minutes and occasionally the clatter of steel coming from the filthy Irish steel mills which occupied over fifty per cent of the island's sixty two acres. When my tour was completed I was replaced by Redmond, and when I rejoined the others inside, the guard commander asked me to proceed to the main billet to check if a certain seaman had returned on the last boat that night. As instructed, I marched into the building and found the chap's bed unoccupied, and so inviting. So, I therefore lay on it and fell fast asleep immediately, and then I was abruptly awoken by Deniffe, who was pulling me, feet first along the wooden floor, towards the main door. He had been ordered to find me, and thankfully, he didn't report back to Horgan that I was asleep when he discovered me, for I was certain to be marched before the CO. When I arrived back at the guardroom, I realised that I had been away for over an hour, and Dinny believed me when I explained that I had searched everywhere for his seaman friend while I was absent. For the remainder of that night I wondered over and over again, would I really shoot anyone in cold blood if they refused to answer my call of "Halt Who Goes There?", the regulation challenge as laid down in standard orders. Anyway thank heavens I survived my first really important undertaking in the service.

The following day for us was referred to as "resting off", and I slept like a log throughout the day despite the fact that (as I was informed later) some of the other occupants in the room were playing poker on my bunk for a short period while I rested. That evening, when everyone was gone ashore chasing women and drink, I decided to remove my No 1 uniform from the locker, and press and clean every inch of the two piece outfit. Then I washed the blue jean collar and silk scarf, and polished my issue black shoes until I could see the reflection of my face in the toes of them. All this great attention to detail was because on the following Friday morning, I was heading up to the capital city in my finest rigout with everything in perfect shape.

But first for the next two days I was to accompany PO Paddy Brown to monitor the condition of the heavy ship's ammunition, which was stored on Spike Island, along with an extremely large amount of depth charges which were packed with heavy explosives. Paddy Brown was a born serviceman, who had served in our Army, the British Army, and the Police, and the Palestine Police Force. Obviously, he dressed immaculately, and acted as a professional military person at all times. The following morning, we caught the regular ferry over to Spike at 9.15am, and after a ten minute trip we arrived at this very historical place, and after a short walk we reached the impregnable Fort Mitchel, named after the Irish patriot, John Mitchel, who served time there as a prisoner, before being shipped to Bermuda to serve a term of fourteen years for political offences. In his jail journal, he recalled "that it was a raw, damp, June morning, that I took my last look at Ireland. The First Lieutenant of the ship, Scourge, which was to transport me to Bermuda, arrived in full uniform to remove me to his ship with a boatload of Marines".

Spike Island itself is roughly one hundred acres, and in earlier times, it was a Holy Island, and an anchorage for smugglers. On the 25th of October, 1790, the Lord Lieutenant, the Earl of Westmoreland visited the island, and the fort then being constructed was named "Fort Westmoreland". Around the island, over 100 guns were mounted as protection. In 1806, an army barracks was erected. Then in 1847, the year of the famine, it was opened as a Convicts' Colony for British and Irish prisoners, and in 1850, over 2000 inmates were held there under savage conditions. Mitchel arrived there in May 1848. Then in 1883, all convicts were withdrawn and dispatched to Mountjoy Prison in Dublin, and the island was returned to military control. From that period, Spike remained as the British Headquarters for the South Irish Coastal Defence, until our army took control on July 11th, 1938. Lt Col RHA Love, Royal Artillery, Officer commanding the south of Ireland Coastal Defence, handed over Spike Island to Major P Maher, on behalf of our government, and at 20.50 hours, the Taoiseach, Mr De Valera, raised the tricolour on the main mast.

In the 1950s PO Brown and myself marched across the wooden bridge which stretches across the mote, that surrounds the granite walls and protects the massive fort which is obviously built on the highest point of the island. Once inside you pass the main guardroom, then through a short courtyard when you meet the parade ground, which is usually referred to as the "Square", for it is normally that shape. The barrack rooms again, as is usually the case, surrounds the square. We simply ignored the Army personnel who were stationed there, but I did observe very clearly that they dressed very untidily, casually, and some looked downright unclean. We proceeded through the compound until we reached an old storehouse, which didn't admit any sunlight or dampness, and according to Brown, the temperature remained the same throughout the entire year. Despite that assurance, he automatically checked the gauges, to confirm his assessment. I inspected the huge store used for the very heavy shells for the corvettes six inch guns, which according to Brown (the expert gunnery NCO), had a range of seven miles. Then I checked out the two pounders, or Pom-Pom shells, suitable for the ships' gun placed aft. "The gun", he explained, "has a type of lens hood attached to the end of its barrel".

Packed neatly in another room close by were the deadly depth charges, that must have been responsible for the death and destruction of hundreds of German U-Boats, and their young crews during World War Two. For someone who has never seen them, or even tried to lift them, I will explain that they are very similar to an aluminium beer barrel, but very much heavier, since they are loaded with high explosive charges, and the casing is solid steel. They were all placed on timber beams, and set in rows of several hundreds, and all were painted in the Naval Services, battleship grey shade. One of those deadly devices were to play a major role on the corvette, *Cliona* in a few years' time, but I can only explain that incident later in this narrative. What also caught my attention during my two day visit was that the billets and the steel stairs leading up to the upper rooms, were in an extremely dangerous shape. The cookhouse's drainage system was stuffed, and the waste water was returning through a manhole within the cookhouse itself. An incinerator burning rubbish nearby was responsible for filling the cookhouse with foul smelling black smoke, when the wind blew from the west. The canteen and the messes were dirty and untidy. The army disbanded the coastal defence in 1979, and the Navy then took over, and attempted to make the island habitable, but during the car joyriding epidemic in 1984, the government panicked and dumped them on Spike and reopened the place as a prison, and on seeing the state of the place, the prisoners immediately set the entire establishment on fire one Saturday night. The complex was rebuilt for convicted criminals at a cost of many millions of pounds, which included televisions and videos, a choice of food at meal times, and central heating! What a shame, because between 1938 (when the British departed) and 1979 (when our Army abandoned the site), no maintenance of any sort was carried out to improve the living conditions for servicemen who volunteered their services for their country.

Friday finally came, and without waiting for the

base's pipe, I jumped out of bed at seven and commenced the long and enjoyable process of getting washed and dressed for going ashore, which is totally unlike dressing up for the CO's parade. The others were slagging the life out of me, with remarks like "Keep away from the women, because in that get-up, they won't be able to resist you!" Muxer again joined in, and shouted out so all could hear, that bellbottom trousers were not designed to dispose of them if the ships sink. "They are for quick disposal, if you meet the right bird", and he added, "Don't come back to this fucking billet with a dose of VD because we don't want it!" I immediately dressed in my uniform, and asked Stretch to remove all dust and pieces of grey wool from the billets' blankets from the back of my tunic, and after satisfying myself in the washhouse mirrors that I was fit to go ashore, I rushed and caught the motor launch, Sir Cecil Romer which was on duty. She only had a passenger certificate to carry 35 in fine weather, but since it was early morning, it was adequate for this trip. The above vessel along with the Sir John Wyndham, General McHardy, and John Adams, were all named after Secretaries of States to Ireland, and were handed over with Fort Westmoreland (Spike) and the Forts of Carlisle, Templebreedy, and Camden (all in Cork harbour) in 1938.

When I disembarked from the Cecil Romer, I walked directly to the Station, where a train was standing, as they usually are, because all boats out of and into Haulbowline, are arranged to meet the incoming and outgoing trains from Cobh. With the excitement of my first home leave I had completely forgotten to borrow a suitcase to carry my civvy suit and overcoat. All I brought was a service towel, soap, toothbrush, and toothpaste, plus shoe brushes, and a tiny clothes brush for the proper maintenance of the uniform. I was to deeply regret that fatal mistake for many years. On the way up to Cork the remainder of the passengers completely ignored me, which wasn't unusual, for they were well used to seeing naval ratings journeying back and forth from Cork.

When I reached Cork, I had some time at my

disposal, so I therefore visited the CIE bar, and ordered a Carlsberg. As I drank it, I could feel the eyes of a group of strangers to the city (perhaps tourists) staring at the uniform, and on the way to the Dublin train, a young lad of about thirteen asked me was there a French Navy ship in port. I answered that I didn't know, but that it was possible that there was one tied up along the quays. The French naval ratings' walking out uniform is very similar to ours. The immediate difference one would notice is that the bobbin on their caps is red, while ours, although the same size, is blue. On the long trip to Dublin, travelling second class (officers use first class warrants), I really began to notice that most of the others were staring at me, so I was then positive that something was out of place on my No 1, or that I had picked up a very noticeable stain. So when the first available toilet became free I rushed in, locked the door tightly, and stripped everything off and thoroughly examined every inch of it and found all to be in perfect order. Then I looked into the small mirror and said to myself, "What the feckin' hell is wrong with me?" I redressed and returned to my seat, and after about fifteen minutes, the woman sitting across from me, asked me "What navy do you belong to, son?" "The Irish Navy, misses", I answered smartly. But it doesn't say 'Ireland' or 'Irish' on your cap". "No", I again replied, "it says 'Éire'". "I never heard of that name. What does it mean?" "It means Ireland, it's the Irish name for Ireland, misses". "It's nice" she added, while looking me up and down, and then turning to her friend said, "I never knew we had a navy".

Immediatley I started to get a murdering headache, and I sensed that things were beginning to go terribly wrong again. As usual when I receive those feelings, I'm proved right. When we reached Kingsbridge station, I ran across John's Road and caught the 79 bus, while everybody simply stared at me, as if I had three eyes, with one in the centre of my forehead. It was beginning to dawn on my that they were either very impressed with me, and therefore wishing they were me, or more likely I was a figure of wonder, or perhaps fun. When, I jumped off the bus I was left in no doubt for then the slagging from the neighbours' kids was unbelievable, and extremely hurtful. It started with "Hey, you, ye dry land sailor", and "The Irish Navy go home everyday for their dinner". The jeering was coming thick and fast. Another young fellow asked me did I bring him back a parrot. Another said "No, a monkey!" As I walked faster and faster to the safety of our house, a much older man, whom I didn't recognise, started singing a tune I never heard before. I cannot compare the air to anything else, so all I can offer are some of the words that go like this "We have one battle-ship that's true; but we want some better than the Murchu, and now is the time to make a start, with an admiralty, they have the sea, now they've got me, so all they want is a navy, a navy, a jolly old Irish navy". I was sick and devastated after enduring that unmerciful hammering.

When I knocked at our hall door my mother answered and said, with a very surprised look on her face, "Who are you?" "I'm Jim, your son", I replied. "But I thought you joined the merchant navy, and what are you wearing that get up for?" "It's my No 1 dress, mother", I said, with as much emphasis as possible. "And where's the suit I sent you down the money for?" "That's locked up in my steel locker". "You should have brought it up with you, son", she said, with a funny look of concern expressed on her face. "You can't wear that bastern suit around this house, or outside on the road. What about Sunday? you can't go to the church dressed up like a tailor's dummy, Everyone will be looking at us. You better sit in at the fire until it's time for you to go back to Cork. I'm not going to be talked about up here". I felt like a leper, and an outcast, what the hell was I to do?

I sat at the fire while eating a stew that my mother had reheated for me, and evaluated my position which I reckoned was desperate. I couldn't walk about in my uniform, which I knew was clean and attractive. But as I listened to the Bush Radio, Nat King Cole was singing *Mona Lisa*, I had a brain wave: why not ask my father for the loan of his long black crombie overcoat, and then if I discard the hat, I could cover the remainder of the uniform with the overcoat. Of course the only problem was that I couldn't remove the coat in public, no matter how hot the conditions were to become, and the bellbottom trousers would be flapping all over the place, because they were at least twenty eight inches wide. When my father finally decided to return home on his bicycle at about 11pm that night, with a good few pints under his belt, he readily agreed to the use of his coat for whatever purpose, and he added "Anything for my eldest son!" He then went directly to bed, and his snoring was penetrating the ceiling while I planned my next move against the singer, and the source of that disgraceful song about the navy.

The following morning, after a breakfast of porridge and toast covered with stork margarine, (the others used dripping), I took the bus as far as McBirneys. I then made my way up to Waltons in North Frederick Street, and asked the young assistant did he ever hear of a record about the Irish Navy. He looked up a catalogue and instantly said "yes!, it's sung by Jimmy O'Dea, on "His Masters Voice" label and was recorded in London on the 9/5/1938. I thought of strangling O'Dea, and if I could, I would have smashed every one of his ridiculous records, because they were doing dreadful damage to the service. Much later I discovered to my horror, that a music hall comedian named Jack Cruise used the joke about the sailors going home for their dinners, when he was frequently short of good material. Anything for a laugh!

I Join the Flotilla

After mass on Sunday, I decided that I would return to Haulbowline on Monday and cancel my leave, for apart from Ann, I had developed real friendships with several of the lads there, particularly Stretch, Doyler and Hector. On the Tuesday, the divisional officer informed me that on the following Monday, I was being sent out to the L E (Long Éireannach), Irish ship, Maev and little did I know then how rough things were to get out there. In the meantime, I rang Ann at work to explain that I had returned voluntarily from leave to be with her and my friends, and made arrangements to see her again the following Saturday evening outside the Commodore Hotel at 7pm. During that week, it was explained to me that the Maev was due in on Saturday morning at 9am for refuelling, and that myself and Tierney were to join her there at the oil wharf first thing on Monday morning. She was also due to dry-dock in nearby Rushbrooke later that day for minor adjustments to her propeller and rudder and to have her bottom scraped and repainted with redlead based paint, which is now outlawed, because it has been proved dangerous to marine life. Tierney and I then arranged with Army Private O'Meara, whose responsibility was to drive an army tractor and trailer (the only transport on the island), to collect our kits while he was delivering food and other provisions to the ship.

On the following Friday night, Mugu and the other poacher, his young rogue from seaman's branch were surrounded by Fishery officers, who, acting on a tip-off caught the pair of them with a couple of ten pound salmon in peak condition, which were destined for an exclusive restaurant just outside Cobh. When the Fishery officials searched Mugu they found a notebook packed with names and addresses of hotels, pubs and restaurants around the locality, stating how much per pound weight they were prepared to pay for fish, crayfish, and lobsters in their prime. All the establishments as listed in the book were raided and their stocks of illegally procured salmon were removed from their fridges, as evidence to be entered and used for future court appearances. Curiously, Mugu was never charged, although he was questioned at length by the military and civilian police. But what was common knowledge was the fact that he regularly supplied the CO with lobsters for his own table, and that fright didn't discourage him from his illegal activity for he continued his poaching until he retired from the service years later. While we were enjoying our usual break in the civvy canteen during the CO's rounds on

Saturday morning, a few crew members of the Maev, who on being informed that I was to join, volunteered some helpful hints regarding the ship which were to prove very useful for the immediate future. They were:

(1) Don't, no matter how thirsty you become, drink the water on board unless you boil it first.
(2) Never eat any food from the fridge until it's cooked and begins to burn.
(3) Above all, on no account eat anything that originated in the food store without checking every pick of it.

"Why?" asked Stretch. "Why do you think, you stupid fucker!" replied Halligan, "because the room is full of cockroaches, and millions of them are living in the sacks of sugar, custard, and porridge. The other day, the cook forgot to inspect the rice before cooking it, and only when we were served the stuff in the messes was it discovered that the cockroaches were cooked along with the rice. McCluskey, up in the seaman's bunk space congratulated the cook for at last adding what he assumed was currants to the dessert. Pints McEvoy announced that at least they were served some fresh meat". I wondered was all this just bullshit talk, although I did thank them for the valuable information, and requested Tierney to remind me to check out the matter on Monday.

That evening as usual we all descended on the washhouse together to clean up and again attempt shaving with little success, for Paddy McCormack severely cut his upper lip, and Stretch removed a boil and several pimples at one stroke of his safety razor. Think of what he would have achieved with a cut throat in his deadly hands! Brannigan, Chackie White, Whelan and Ginger Dwyer were again arguing over football at the far side of the partition, while Paddy Smith was again practising his singing of the latest Bing Crosby record, but it was difficult to hear over the others' shouting and roaring.

When we finally went out that night, Stretch and

Doyler escorted me over to the Commodore and when Ann spotted the pair of them, she said, "I'm sorry, lads, but I didn't bring my friends with me". Stretch, as was his style, looked curiously at her, but Doyler, as cheeky as ever, said "Why, what are they like and where are they?" "Up in Fords, in Cork", she answered, and the next time we meet, I'll bring them down on the train". "That sounds smashing", remarked Doyler, as he puffed gently on his pipe, and I could almost hear his brain working. We then all decided to enter the hotel for a drink, and as we entered the hall we spotted the Navy's 2IC, Peter Kavanagh along with a number of his card playing friends, and before we reached the bar we were requested to leave. A clear case of blatant discrimination was what Ann called it. and she promised she would ask her father to investigate the matter with a solicitor as soon as humanly possible. The Well House was now the obvious choice and as we approached the building, it became clear that the proprietor had again returned from hospital, for the place was packed to the ceiling upstairs and downstairs with intoxicated customers absolutely enjoying themselves, and no doubt celebrating the owner's return to full health. Since it was a beautiful summer's evening, we decided to join in the festivities, and I whispered to Ann that I really didn't mind missing another classical music lesson on just this occasion. We then managed to smuggle out a table and four chairs. Then we ordered our drinks and sat alongside the quay wall for the entire evening admiring the panoramic view of the magnificent harbour, and watched the steam ships coming from and going to foreign destinations. Much later we were all invited into the home of a local couple, Ollie and Rose McKiernan, for a late night supper. During a few moments alone with Ann, I explained to her that I was due to sail the following week, and it could be some time before we could meet again. She asked me to write as often as possible, telling her how much I missed her, and that I was always thinking of her, day and night, and not to forget a card and a present for her birthday next month. "OK", I said as I escorted her to her door, and as I departed for the last boat she again reminded me about the card and present. When I told Doyler and Stretch what she had insisted on, they replied that she had me in the palm of her sweet little hand. "Maybe she has", I thought to myself.

The truck driver collected Tierney and myself on the following Monday, and when we loaded up our kits on his trailer, we proceeded over to the supply stores to collect food and bedding for the ship's company. We headed to the oil wharf, and when I took a long look at my new home for many months to come, the *Maev* looked proud and strong, and appeared much bigger than her 205 feet, and much heavier than her 1,020 tons. That was just an illusion, because when I saw her first, the tide was at its highest point, thereby lifting her above the pier and making her seem larger. I also noticed she had a fresh coat of paint on her, and all the brasswork was shining. But despite her smartness and elegance, I knew she was a bloody bitch with no heart, who like her sister ships, all two hundred and fifty seven of them constructed during the war, broke the hearts of every man who sailed on them, and would no doubt break mine too. On further examination of the *Maev*, formerly *HMS Oxlip*, a flower class corvette all named after flowers, my initial reaction was that she certainly looked like a naval vessel. On her bow was mounted a large four inch gun with a range of 4000 metres. There were also two 20mm Oirlikon anti-aircraft guns fitted on each side of the bridge, and a single two pounder Pom-Pom anti-aircraft gun, positioned near the after deck. Also visible were four depth charge throwers, two secured on each side of the deck, plus two depth charge rails placed near the stern to allow them to roll off the ship. I also observed on the starboard side, directly in front of the bridge, the other anti-submarine weapons aboard, which were the Hedgehogs, a sixty-five pound bomb, that was fired far ahead of the ship in a group of twenty four, and if they came in contact with a submarine they could inflict very great damage.

There was activity everywhere on deck, and the first two persons I noticed were CPO, Rory McCarthy, who was supervising the pumping of the water and fuel oil aboard ship, and the famous CPO, Batt Sullivan who had just joined as Coxswain. "Ah", said the Batt to me, "you must be diamond Jim Brady. I knew your namesake in America. He was a terrific guy, and when I get time, I'll tell you about himself and myself. Now, get aboard all those supplies because we're steaming right away up to Rushbrook for a minor refit". Then he shouted louder than any loudhailer, "Quartermaster, pipe hands to harbour stations, and you Chief Stoker McCarthy, are you not finished oiling yet? Within minutes, the fuel and water hoses were disconnected, the gangway was brought on board, and the lines were taken in. The Batt then entered the wheel house to commence his duty as helmsman, and as the ship headed up river very slowly, a young seaman emerged from the wheel house and ran towards the port side, and reported back to the Batt that they had indeed cleared the pier. "What was that all about?", I asked the quartermaster. "Oh", he said, "the Batt doesn't trust the captain or the officers, and when he is at the wheel, he's afraid the ship will collide with the pier or the quay wall and then he would be blamed instead of the shaggin' officers".

Chief McCarthy then escorted me to the stoker's mess deck down steel staircases, through companion ways with steel pipes and valves fitted everywhere. We walked through steel watertight doors that were fitted to all men of war, for safety purposes. The smell was unbearable, for it was a mixture of diesel oil and paraffin oil, of steam and of the toil of almost eighty human beings, that must for months on end, eat, sleep, work and live on a steel vessel, 205'x33'x14' with no air conditioning, and all portholes are tightly shut while the ship is at sea. As we passed the fridge, I could smell the meat, and it was clear that it was deteriorating. From the pool of water lodged underneath the fridge, it was also obvious that the motor badly needed an overhaul, or renewal. The mess itself, where the stoker's branch both ate, and used for recreational purposes was awful. It was just a simple compartment, fitted with a table and benches, along with one radio speaker enclosed in a wooden frame, which had a switch for highering or lowering the sound. But we had no control over what we received because all radios were fitted in the radio room, and that was strictly off limits to all except those employed there. So, for example, if the radio compartment was unoccupied during the weekend, or holiday periods, we were frequently stuck with Radio Éireann, and in those days, their taste was for chamber music, religious music, and quite often plays in the Irish language. That lot went down a bomb, especially when we couldn't turn it off! Chief McCarthy then pointed out a small washhouse, containing five stainless steel sinks, with no stoppers fitted. One seaman was using a piece of newspaper for that purpose. A shower unit was also available, but I was informed that it never actually worked. Water was pumped by hand from the tanks below deck, when required by the seventy ratings using that facility. Slightly aft of that compartment, were the toilets, and this area was the most degrading part of the vessel, because placed inside were five toilet bowls facing each other, with no doors fitted to any of them. So, as you conducted your bodily functions, the others were watching you, and vice versa. The only ventilation to that horrible place was one open porthole. Some crew members who rather than suffer the humiliation of using that facility, chose certain other parts around the ship, most notably, behind the main boilers. They were simply too ashamed to undertake their natural necessities, while others were present.

Next, we inspected the seamen's mess deck, which unfortunately, included their eating, sleeping and recreational facilities combined into one room, an approximate area of twelve feet by twenty feet. Their wooden kit lockers were used for various purposes, such as seating at meal times, placing mattresses on for sleeping, and of course, their intended use as storage for their uniforms and accessories. Hammocks were hanging at various points around the area, along with bunk beds fitted in pairs, left me with the impression that the unfortunate lads resembled sardines pressed into a tin can. Their sleeping accommodation overflowed into another cramped compartment below, where several more rows of bunk beds were hooked onto the bulkhead on each side of the ship. Below that again, was the anchor chain locker where the chain was stored while at sea, and that rattled out a deafening noise with the movement of the vessel. The stokers' sleeping quarters were just aft of that, and this was a room of about 10x10 feet to house about thirty personnel, again in bunk beds. No ventilation was available here, except the stairway opening situated approximately mid way across the deck. Below us again were the fresh water tanks that supplied the ship's needs.

There were no cooking facilities whatsoever fitted aboard, not even a kettle for making a cup of tea, and no hot presses for keeping food warm in any of the messes. Therefore, it was apparent that all food was cooked in the ship's galley, and then distributed from there. I was shocked and horrified that it was impossible, according to Rory, to have anything to eat, after the galley was locked after tea was served at 4pm each day. "That regulation needs changing", I thought to myself, "and there has to be a way around that minor difficulty". Perhaps there is a locksmith as a crew member? Later, I would investigate the remainder of the vessel. In the meantime, we were approaching the dock, and as we entered it the huge dock door was immediately closed behind us, and as the water was pumped out, large wooden beams were placed between the wall of the dry dock and the ship's side, both port and starboard, to hold the vessel steady and in line as the area was emptied of water. When that was completed, the workers commenced erecting scaffolding without delay, and then the hammering and drilling along the hull started, and the effects of that were felt everywhere aboard the ship. But the most annoying aspect of being in dry-dock was that we couldn't use the toilets or the washing facilities on board, because everything would flush out on top of the workmen below. Therefore, we were forced to use the dockyard washhouse and toilets ashore, and they were utterly filthy and disgraceful. Some of our crew members simply didn't bother washing for the two days we were in, and used the toilet facilities in the local public bar.

My next task was to inquire as to who the captain was. Somebody answered that his name was Lt-Cmdr William Anthony Murray, generally known by all as "Wam", who along with Lt-Cmdr Harry Henry were the first ever cadets recruited for the naval service in December 1946, when both completed an extended naval officer's course in the Royal Naval College Dartmouth, in England. The executive officer was another cadet who underwent the International Midshipman's Training at the Britannia School in 1950. He was Lt the "Yank" O'Mahony, the man who distinguished himself the night the young rating jumped over the side of the passenger launch. This was a highly skilled individual who knew his job extremely well, and carried out his duties with absolute professionalism, and dedication, and from all accounts the crews of all the ships he sailed on held him in the highest regard. Therefore, I was delighted to sail under him.

My direct boss was Lt "Snags" Sutton whom I mentioned earlier as the officer who insisted on all empty glasses being left on the table in the mess, in order to check and count the number he had taken before he left. Snags was the engineering officer, and for all the years I knew him, I never actually saw him with a spanner in his hands, although I once observed him standing in white overalls. He was however, well qualified, having served in the Indian Navy before entering our service, but he never got involved in the job. Instead, he simply took the best advice his NCOs could offer, and frequently stood over them while they worked. He was very fortunate to have as his chief engine room artificer, Joseph "Jock" Taft a fellow Scotchman, who knew the corvette's main engine and auxiliary machinery inside out, for he had served his apprenticeship and then worked for many years in John Brown's shipyard, Greenock, where most of the corvettes were constructed. (Some were built in Canada). Chief Taft's dedication and knowledge greatly helped to extend the lifetime of the ships, and successive engineering officers were greatly indebted to him for sharing his skills and knowledge. The boatswain, or bosun, was the delightful Kerry Byrnes, another highly skilled seaman, who received great respect because of his total commitment to his task of supervising the maintenance and upkeep of the vessel in all weathers. We had professional personnel in key positions operating the ship, and for that at least I was thankful.

Later, as I observed the dockyard men working under the ship, I noticed that they were able to remove sections of the wood which the ship's keel was resting on, to enable them access to whatever section of the vessel that required immediate attention or inspection. The Maev was extremely quiet that night because most crew members had gone ashore, and all machinery was closed down, simply because no water coolants were now available. In the seamen's mess another marathon poker game was taking place, which included Thunder, whom I referred to earlier and a few others. The topic of conversation was as usual women at the top of the list, and what they would do to a few of them if they dared step aboard; what they thought of certain officers, which was mostly unprintable. But one old hand related an incident that took place when the Macha, under the command of Lt-Cmdr, Petie Kavanagh visited foreign ports, which included Stockholm, Amsterdam, Portsmouth, Fishguard, and Antwerp, during June and July 1954. As the ship docked in Antwerp, the executive officer warned the crew members to keep out of the notorious sinful Skipper Street, no matter what happened. Later, while they were ashore, a group who had consumed a large quantity of beer decided to be adventurous and visit the street of sin, for a taste of the good life. The innocent Irish lads entered a night club and were amazed to find beautifully dressed "ladies" sitting around just waiting to be asked to dance. Our lads duly obliged. But as they danced closer and closer, they noticed that the ladies' breasts were moving around from side to side, inside their clothing, and that those females had male genitals. The fighting Irish then started a row and demanded their money back, but the jealous customers and their boyfriends who were admiring the dancers kicked out the ship's crew members on to the street.

Pints McEvoy then explained that while they were in Amsterdam, a very young stoker had made a date with a young lady early one evening. But unexpectedly, and at the last moment he was ordered to clean out the bilges, an extremely dirty and oily area underneath the ship's boilers. When he finally finished that undertaking he did not have adequate time to properly clean every part of his body, so since his feet were the dirtiest, he simply wore a thick pair of clean stockings to cover the oily dirt, and contain the smell. When he eventually got ashore, they visited various night clubs and bars, and then returned to her apartment. When they decided to go to bed, he stripped everything off except the stockings. Despite her insistence he refused to remove them, explaining to her that it was an old Irish custom to make love while the stockings covered the feet.

And so the yarns continued. Someone else said, "do you remember what happened when we went to Stockholm?" "Oh, yeah, we were given a tour of the brewery, and our lot were asked would they like to sample the beer. They sampled it alright", said McEvoy "they nearly drank the place dry, and after several hours sampling they couldn't walk, or even stand, and a private bus had to be hired to return them to the ship!" He continued: "Despite being footless, they were still able to load up a consignment of beer into the compartment of the bus that was reserved for passenger luggage". "Yeah", continued McCluskey, "It took us nearly fifteen minutes to unload the booze that evening onto the ship, and the Macha smelled like a brewery all the way back. Pinhead, while dealing the cards, asked did anyone recall the trip *Macha* made with Lt CJ "Titch" Byrne, back in 1951 to Brest and Vigo in Spain. He explained that after a group of the lads were eventually thrown out of a bar in Spain after a row, they were so drunk that when they reached the town's centre they decided to take a nap on the street's wooden benches. All except two woke up during the night and made their way back to the ship. But when the others woke up, the town's people were making their way to work, and a large crowd had gathered around our navy lads to admire them for they were completely naked, as their clothes and all their belongings had been removed from them while they were sleeping it off. Both of them begged a loan of a pair of shorts each for the journey back to the ship, while trying to hide their embarrassment. "And do you know what?" said Kerry Byrnes, two officers were carried aboard that night pissed drunk, and both were howling to a full moon.

That conversation continued for the best part of an hour but after a while I refused to listen, because in most company they tended to exaggerate, and it was therefore impossible to tell fact from fiction. So I turned in and despite its ugliness and untidiness, the bunk bed was surprisingly rather comfortable, and with my height and fitness, it was easy to reach the top bunk. The following morning even though we were in a dockyard surrounded by civilian workers, naval drill and routine was not relaxed, and at 7.45am we were ordered to fall in on the upper deck for inspection, counting, and the detailing of duty for the day. I was dispatched to the senior NCO's mess down aft as messman to the CPOs and POs, and as I made my way down I said to myself, "they must have been waiting for me". When I entered it, the place was as primitive and basic as the others on the vessel. It was roughly ten feet by five feet, with a wooden table placed in the centre, and wooden benches situated at each side, with a dark green leatherette upholstery. Lying asleep on one of the benches and covered with two brown army blankets was PO Cook Paddy Kennedy, the man I referred to earlier, who was caught in the base's cookhouse stirring the tea with the handle of the brush by the visiting army Colonels. Anyway, I tried as best I could not to disturb him, for he appeared much older than my own father.

However, the Batt entered the room, complaining

about how close the captain brought the ship to striking the quay wall while entering the dock the previous afternoon. Almost immediately, he was joined by CPO Taft and McCarthy, PO Johnnie O'Brien, Padge Farrelly, and the bosun, overhearing the Batt's remark brought up the subject of a very serious incident involving the same ship, that we were now serving on. The subject was discussed in great detail by all who were present, and while I served them their porridge, and toasted their bread on the tiny electric fire, I learned that while the ship was entering the Alexandra Basin in Dublin, the acting Engineering Officer, warrant officer, Timmy Gillan was in his bunk when he should have been at his post in the engine room. However, they went on to reveal that the telegraph instructions from the bridge to the engine room were either sent or received arse ways, and the orders for "Slow Astern!" changed to "Slow Ahead!", "Half Astern!" to "Half Ahead!" and "Full Astern!" to "Full Ahead!" Then, inevitably, the ship plowed into the granite basin, going full ahead, and destroyed the entire bow of the ship, resulting in months of dry-docking for repairs, costing very many thousands of pounds. Now I was beginning to understand the Batt's nervousness and reluctance to trust the captains on the bridge, because that above incident only occured a few years previously. Later, I was to discover that the collision with the quay wall was responsible for a large degree of edginess, especially within the engine room senior personnel, who took particular care of their responsibilities, especially when entering and leaving harbours.

While they chatted, smoked and finished their meal, I decided to investigate another section of the ship that concerned me in the immediate area. Just outside the mess on the after deck, I entered a steel hatch and dropped into a compartment containing a huge diesel engine of approximately four hundred and fifty horse power, and it was evident from the electrical switch gear that this machine was the electricity generator for the ship's requirements. It was switched off because no water coolants were available in dry dock. The place was reeking with the stench of diesel oil which covered the deck, the bulk heads and the engine itself. It was clear then, even while the engine was stopped that this was a very unpleasant place to be. Just aft of that I forced myself through another steel opening and discovered a second nasty location containing a system called a Telemoter, that works and controls the rudder movements, which were obviously directed from the wheelhouse directly under the bridge. That system was of course not operating then, but I shall refer to both that and the generator later. The main engine room was situated below and slightly forward of the NCO's tiny sleeping accommodation. The engine room appeared gigantic and very complicated when I first entered it, and as I made my way down to the lower deck to inspect the 2,759 Horse Power steam reciprocation four cylinder triple expansion engine, a very attractive brass plate explained that the engine was made by John C Kinkade Greenock. The engine was connected to one shaft, and later I learned that the maximum speed was 16 knots and the cruising speed was 12 knots. I further investigated and discovered two steam operated electricity generators, and a condencer for returning waste steam back into water. I checked out the gear mechanism for moving the engine forward and astern, the telegraph controls linking the bridge with the engine room and a voice pipe, a very effective means of communicating by shouting through a copper piping, linking key areas of the ship. For instance, from the bridge to the wheelhouse and from the boiler room to the engine room, and from there back to the bridge, where various orders would be directed from, concerning speed (or the lack of it), and frequently complaints about the boiler room making black smoke which in a war-time situation, would give your position away easily to aircraft or another vessel.

When I returned to the mess to wash the dishes and clean up, they were about to leave, and as the chief, ERA Joe Taft stopped to re-light his pipe, I asked him why PO Kennedy was sleeping in the mess, and why a bunk space was not available. "Well you know son", he said, "Paddy shouldn't be out here at all, and there is no appointment for a PO Cook on any of the ships at sea. So, since there's no job for him, there's no accommodation in the bunk space. What's more", he added, "he hates the Exec, Yank Mahony, because he thinks he is responsible for his posting on to the ship. But the Yank told me that he was ordered by the base CO to take poor Paddy even though the Yank strongly protested, saying that the ship was already carrying a full compliment of 78.

That evening, while they were having their tea in the mess, some of the younger POs were complaining about how difficult things were concerning living conditions aboard ship, and the Batt in typical form replied that they didn't know nor could they ever really understand how grim life could really be. Then he related to a captive audience how, while prospecting for gold in the Klondike, it was so fucking cold that:

(1) They had to thaw their words out to hear themselves talking.
(2) The flame of the candle froze inside the tent.
(3) When he and his fellow gold prospectors went outside to relieve themselves, the urine froze before it reached the ground, and therefore, they had to break it away from their bodies.

Then he lit his pipe and said, "Diamond Jim Brady, go and make your cox'n a nice cup of fresh tea, and I'll tell you about Chicago in 1932" As I said earlier in this narrative, this Naval Service is better than any university, because it instructs you in life and people. The Batt was one of Ireland's great eccentrics, and he was known far and wide, and the greatest statement ever made about him was that, while visiting the Vatican for an audience with the Pope, somebody said, "who's that with the Batt Sullivan?"

I cleaned up quickly and returned to my own mess for tea, because I was not allowed to dine in another area, and while chatting and listening to the Radio Éireann news, Willie Mynes mentioned to me that he found a spare key to fit the Galley door. "Things are definitely looking up", I said to myself. I then confided to Willie that I heard that the potato locker on deck could be easily opened, because the lock is faulty and requires replacing. We then decided that later on, when the officers went ashore, we would force open the potato cage, then open the galley and fry a big pan of chips, and brew up a big pot of tea, just like porter. While I peeled the spuds, Mynes lit the torch and dropped the flame into the diesel oil operated cooker and immediately the entire unit burst into flames and exploded with a huge bang, which shocked and rattled the entire ships. Several workers on overtime below the ship thought that the fuel and ammunition on board had exploded. They jumped off their scaffolding, and in their scramble to escape up the steps of the dry-dock, two of them were severely injured. We simply grabbed everything belonging to ourselves, and despite our blackened faces and singed hair and eyebrows, we rushed back to our bunkspace and commenced cleaning ourselves up.

What actually caused the problem was that the previous occupant of the galley had forgotten to turn off the fuel to the burner, and the furnace had filled up with oil and gases, and when we lit it, the mixture ignited and exploded. The duty PO ERA was sent for to examine the cooker, and found that several steel bolts holding the unit to the bulkhead had been sheered off. Its exhaust system was cracked, the main fuel supply line to it was broken, and the brackets holding the burner unit to the oven were buckled. "The entire cooker", he declared, "could be repaired for use at breakfast time, with a little help from the dockyard employees". Curiously, he diagnosed everything as being an accident, because there was no evidence of a break in, and he assumed that the oven ignited itself, due to the build up of gases in the cooker, which remained hot long after use. After that adventure the pair of us retired to the local dock bar and ordered a few drinks to calm down the nerves and listened to a group singing and playing traditional Irish music, and plotted our strategy and prepared answers to questions from the captain, in case we were spotted running away from the scene, and then reported to the officer of the day. We heard nothing further and there the matter rested.

The following evening, we were due to leave this place, and at the first opportunity I would have a decent wash, and scrub my overalls with a scrubbing brush (the only means possible then). When the moment finally came, everything was performed in reverse order for leaving the dry-dock. First the water was allowed in slowly through openings in the dock gate, and after some time the entire door was opened. Then as the ship began to float, the timber beams (similar to telegraph poles) were removed by crane and placed on the quay wall. With the captain on the bridge, and the officer of the watch on duty, the coxswain in the wheelhouse, wireless operator in position, the signal's man standing by in case flags may be required to communicate with other vessels, and a full deck crew are also at their posts. Below in the engine room, the engineer was standing close to the engine's controls, along with the Chief ERA and the duty PO ERA, plus the greaser to log all the ship's movements direct from the bridge. Forward in the boiler rooms, three men were also awaiting their orders to raise steam. Everybody was therefore in place, and the vessel was ready to leave the dock. The ship moved astern with the help of her Capstan fitted on the after deck. When she had cleared that locality, she was then helped to manoeuvre herself towards the main channel of the river Lee by a small harbour tug.

When she reached that position, she continued down river under her own steam, now towards Haulbowline on her starboard side, then Spike Island. At this stage, the deck crew including a junior officer, were standing on the ship's port side facing the town of Cobh, an ancient custom, to show that her guns were unarmed, and therefore posed no threat to the port. We then passed the Ormonde Cinema, where I hoped very soon to return with Ann, hand in hand. Then also on our port side, we passed the famous Holy grounds, once the site of a British army establishment, and further down I inspected the harbour area that was retained at one stage as a quarantine station for visiting foreign ships, until it was established that there was no danger of spreading diseases to the inhabitants of the region. Then we turned ninety degrees to starboard to clear the Spit Bank lighthouse that was once manned by two men. The Spit warns of a highly dangerous sandbank. To our port I viewed Aghada then Whitegate, where the country's only oil refinery is now constructed. As we proceeded towards the mouth of the harbour Fort Camden was pointed out to me, plus the entrance to Crosshaven.

As we steamed towards the massive white structure of Roches Point lighthouse, the vessel started to pitch and roll despite the fact that it was summer, and we had not yet left the shelter of the harbour. As we approached the Daunt lightship, just outside the mouth of the harbour, I asked a crew member where we were heading to. "Well", he said, "if we turn to port we're going east, and if we sail to starboard, it's the west coast". "Yes", I answered, "but where exactly are we sailing to?" "I don't know, because we are never told by the captain or the other officers". "But", I continued, "has the captain in his possession sealed orders in a brown envelope with a harp printed on it, and a typed directive stating 'For the Captain's Eyes Only', Top Secret?" "I don't know", he again repeated. "What a bloody stupid situation", I said to myself. Here we are sailing around the coast of Ireland during peacetime on fishery protection patrol, policing a three mile exclusive zone, looking for foreign fishermen attempting to steal our fish. Nobody, except a few officers, out of a crew of about eighty seven, and all volunteers, know where we were heading, or for how long, or what ports we may visit, or even the duration of the entire patrol Everybody, except the chosen few were left guessing. What a farce! However, we headed up the west coast.

As we left the Daunt astern, the bloody bitch started to roll and pitch violently, even though there was only a force six wind blowing, and it was a bright summer's day. She rolled just like a barrel, as I knew she would after inspecting her back in dry-dock when I realised that indeed she was shaped similarly to a fat barrel. When she pitched the entire ship rattled, and during this, my first experience aboard them, I imagined that when the bow dived into the waves, it would fail to return and that the entire ship would sink, and all the crew would be drowned. It did of course return to the surface, only to dive time after time, hour after hour, and when she rolled, the ship made the complete roll right over from side to side until both sides almost scooped up the sea at either side, and throughout all this I was in complete agony, for I was also over the side where I lost my breakfast and dinner the first time. I spewed over the gunnel of the vessel. I was dying, and I said to myself over and over "Why the hell didn't I join the army, or better still, stay at home with the mother!" The ship was acting like a crazy wild horse, being broken in by a cowboy at a rodeo. It was jumping, shaking, rattling, and diving into the water sideways, then righting herself, and then repeating the motion in reverse order. Not only was she a bitch, she was a mad whore who was out to murder all the men aboard her!

Even though I was dying a thousand deaths, and convinced that I was about to lose all my intestines and some other vital organs, even my heart to the hungry seagulls, who always seem to follow ships, looking for food amongst the garbage, I did somehow get a glimpse of the Old Head of Kinsale. Just ahead of us, I could make out the famous Fastnet Rock. Then the Batt, who had only emerged from the wheelhouse said, "Diamond Jim, isn't it great sailing weather we're having? Sure it's marvellous steaming on a day like this, with plenty of sunshine and fresh air, and beautiful clean sea around us. Yes, it's just like a summer cruise. People would pay dearly for such a trip" If I had a pistol, I would have blown his head off, because I wouldn't have cared, for I was convinced I was about to drop dead. "Now" he continued, "go and collect our teas up in the Galley. I hear there's a fantastic meal of rashers, pudding, sausages, and eggs, plus fry bread for everybody". Just as he finished, I almost got sick into his face and ran to the side to force more valuable fluid from my body. "Ah" said the Batt, "you must have had a feed of porter last night, and they stuck you with a pint of ullage. That's slops you know. Some of them publicans are gangsters. Be careful where you drink. Bring down the grub to the mess, and we'll have a feed of good wholesome food".

When I entered the galley, the cook and the other messmen were smoking cigarettes while they were receiving their quotas of rations, and I was shocked that the ship's violent movements weren't bothering them. As casually as I could, I mentioned the weather to "Pints" and he replied that it was now flat calm, and that I should wait until we met a gale, or until the winter when nobody was allowed on deck, and those who must venture onto the deck for an important reason had to wear a safety harness around their waists, or a rope tied around them, in case they were swept overboard. "My God", I murmured to myself, "I'm really in big trouble now! These ships are going to destroy me, because I shall never get accustomed to this continuous murderous motion. I collected the NCO's food and somehow, perhaps with the help of God, I managed to serve their meal without actually getting sick inside their dining area. But as I got a smell of the eggs, I rushed out onto the after deck, and lost whatever remained inside me, over the stern between the two depth charge rails. I then decided to remain on deck for I was, even at this early stage, beginning to realise that the smell of the various areas of the ship was playing its part in my seasickness agony, along with of course, the maddening rhythm of the vessel's movements. So, I therefore waited until the mess was emptied before I returned to clean up the saucepans and other dishes and restore everything into their rightful place.

As I stood on the after deck again, Kerry Byrnes explained the Fastnet to me, saying that it's often called 'The Eye of Europe' or 'The Teardrop of Ireland' because it's the first piece of land you see on returning across the atlantic, and the last piece of Ireland you see as you are about to leave. He added that it's generally so rough around the slate rock, that it's only possible to land there by boat a few times a year. He added that it's reasonably easy to navigate around the Irish coast, because all you need to do is follow and recognise all the lighthouses which are listed on the charts, and that every lighthouse is an individual, and it's identified by the number of times its lights flash per minute. "I'll remember that Kerry" I replied, "when I purchase my luxury yacht!" The bitch, Maev was still rolling and pitching like hell but life goes on, and a full watch is still in position. The only difference is that they change every four hours. So it's four hours on and eight hours off, and that time off is strictly yours, and you may do as you please, but once on duty you cannot leave your post unless you have been relieved, which is of course the proper procedure that makes for a very safe ship at sea.

As we steamed further and further up the west coast we changed course occasionally to check the nationality of various trawlers that we encountered. None were boarded or searched, but as I passed the radio room below the bridge, I could hear the radio traffic taking place between the fishing fleets and our patrol vessel, presumably reporting the sightings of foreign vessels. I asked the Batt what were the small group of rocks ahead, and he then explained to me that they were the Bull, the Cow, and the Calf. The Bull is the biggest of the three, and the one that was flashing. "And do you know, Diamond Jim, she is over 300 feet high, and 600 feet in diameter, and what's more, there's a huge opening under her where you could sail a small ship under. Yes, lad" he continued, "sure without them no ships would be safe around our coastline. Now, go up to our little canteen and ask for an ounce of tobacco for the cox'n, and tell them I'll pay for it on Friday right after pay parade". "Is it yachtsman you want, Cox?" "Ah, it doesn't matter, lad" he said, "just ask for plug tobacco for meself". Then he added "We're about to enter a place close to me heart, a lovely fishing port, called Castletownbere". I didn't care at that time where we went, even to hell as long as that ship's motion ceased. We entered a huge inlet surrounded by mountains and beautiful scenery and anchored some distance from the town, and as we turned with the tide

I could observe that this was indeed an extremely busy fishing station. Therefore, it was the obvious place to remain for the night and advertise the fact to the trawlermen that the navy was present in their area and attending to their needs. I was so glad to be at last standing on a steady surface, that I even considered visiting the captain to thank him personally for bringing in the ship to a safe haven, where the vessel stays steady while at anchor. I was then so exhausted after such a gruelling day, that I had a quick wash and went straight to bed, and fell asleep immediately.

When I departed for duty the following morning, I overheard the bosun telling the others, including the Batt, that his stores were broken into the night before, and that several tins of battleship grey and white paint were missing, and that around the ship's bunkspaces a large number of oilskins and seaboots were also misplaced, possibly stolen. "That's them fucking fishermen", said the Batt. "I saw the hungry shaggers talking to our shore boat crew last night, when I went across for a few pints, and when I speak to the captain, I'll tell him to board and arrest every trawler, Irish or foreign, if it's painted the same colour of our ship". I later heard in my own mess that the goods were sold for cash with a few lobsters thrown in.

While the Batt and company were finishing their breakfast the boilers were flashed (started up), and then the main engine was turned over for an hour to allow it to heat up before it was needed for duty, because we were heading to sea again at 9am. Just before we left, the diesel generator was closed down, and the two steam operated ones in the engine room were brought into commission to replace it and produce the ship's electricity. When we left the harbour and reached the open sea we headed straight into a westerly gale, and the order went out to last everything down. The ship again started rolling and pitching violently, and before we could secure a rope around the forty gallon oil drums, which held diesel oil and diesel lubracation oil, they started to roll violently around the well deck and the after deck. Chief McCarthy then ordered me to the engine room, to fetch an axe for him to puncture the runaway barrels and empty their contents to prevent them from damaging parts of the ship, or endangering people's lives. I was of course continuing to die of seasickness, but that is no excuse for a crew member aboard ship, because your allocated duties must be carried out. As we steamed further up the coast, the weather continued to deteriorate, and when I visited my own mess, Dermo Kelly said that he heard we were sailing all day and night, but he didn't know exactly where we would be, but based on previous patrols, it might be Killybegs for the weekend. Just as he finished speaking the entire ship started to rattle violently and I could feel that she was gathering speed. I walked forward to the boiler room, and looked down and observed three men below working flat out in a temperature of about 100 degrees Fahrenheit, changing to larger fuel sprayers for the furnaces, speeding up the oil pumps to their fullest working capacity, and opening up the fans to help with the combustion of the fuel. The noise was deafening, and you could only communicate by hand signals, so since I couldn't hear or understand anything there, I rushed back on deck and asked a passing seaman were we under attack, or going into battle to prevent an enemy submarine or destroyer entering our territorial waters. "No", he said, "we are going full ahead because we've spotted a foreign fishing boat some miles ahead".

When we finally approached and surrounded the deadly enemy, I observed that we had in fact trapped an unfortunate thirty five foot wooden lobster boat, with a few French trawlermen aboard looking haggard dirty and unshaven, and obviously quite hungry for they were biting large chunks from a lump of bread similar to a Vienna roll. They had aboard their tiny boat which was isolated from us for minutes at a time, because of the high seas, a large number of lobster pots stored on every available part of the boat. Indeed, some were hanging over the sides, and around her mast. Presumably they were preparing to place them in shallow waters close to our coastline. But since they were not actually fishing, and since no evidence was obtained to indicate that they had placed any lobster pots, they were not arrested or boarded to be searched. The Frenchies then made their way towards our vessel, offering our crew samples of their catch of lobsters and crayfish, that were gratefully accepted, and placed into a large bath of salt water to await consumption over the weekend. When I saw their faces as they handed over their harvest, the tiredness and the effects of three weeks hardship aboard such a tiny craft was clearly evident, and I remarked to the others beside me that they are only trying to make a living and have sailed a long way and just look at the weather they are working in. Where were our fishermen now who moan about foreigners fishing our waters, in the pubs no doubt!

We continued our patrol up the coast at cruising speed, and after I had collected and served the senior NCOs their dinner, Kerry Byrnes escorted me out to the after deck, and again pointed out another famous lighthouse, this time it was Skellig Michael a rock ten miles from the Kerry coast and seven hundred feet high. "And do you know what?" Kerry continued, "monks once lived on that place for a thousand years". The Batt, who was listening said, they were the original Kerrymen, and that his ancestors were born on that rock, and it was the original island of Saints and scholars. I was still dying of seasickness and was therefore, unable to follow the conversation, so I decided to head up to our bunkspace, and try and lie down for a while. But to make matters really worse, as I walked past the heads (toilets), I was informed that we in the stokers division were to lay down our kits in the regulation military manner on our bunks for inspection by the Exec, Lt the Yank O'Mahony. Brochelbank said, "that fucking bollix must be mad, because how can we manage to lay down our gear properly with the ship standing on her shagging head?" It was done because as I later learned, this was just like training division with Ferriter, and is part of the test to see how much you can really take before you crack-up, desert, or buy yourself out. We struggled through sheer torture removing everything from the kit boxes, then pressing and shaping them and presenting every item of clothing in the best possible way.

After approximately an hour, the Yank finally entered the bunkspace while we were all standing firmly to attention, and to our bitter disappointment, he only glanced at each man's kit and then left to return to the officer's wardroom. Psychological warfare, O'Malley called it. We steamed on and on, zig zagging at times maybe, as an exercise for the young officers on the bridge, and with the wind blowing hard from the west, she rolled at an even quickening rate, and we were therefore unable to stand or walk without holding on to some solid object. During tea time in the mess, chief Taft confirmed that the captain told him he would require additional engine room and boiler room personnel for an all night patrol that night, because the vessel was going to undergo a darkened ship operation, which means that all lights except their legitimate navigational lights were to be extinguished, and all port holes were to be firmly closed to eliminate any light from the ship. Pints and McCluskey agreed that this was another naval exercise the officers had learned from the Royal Navy over in Dartmouth perhaps on battleships, and were now trying out that manoeuvre on our punts. "Maybe they are heading back to try and capture that poor French lobster boat laying their pots", added Redmond. "They can do what they like", I said, "because after lights out I'm going to the bunk, because the mess, the Jacks, washhouses, and everywhere else will be stinking with all the portholes closed and no fresh air entering the ship".

Early the next morning, I went on deck for some fresh air and to admire the rugged scenery of our exposed west coast. Apart from the bridge crew and the helmsman whom I could not see, I was the only other person above deck. As I looked across to the horizon, I discovered that for very many miles we were the only ship to be seen, and not even an Irish fishing craft was harvesting the seas. Yet here we were policing our 2,000 mile coastline year after year in all weathers to protect our fisheries from foreign poachers, even though our own fishermen refuse to fish in our exclusive zone. However, since it was Friday and payday, I was told we were anchoring early in a place called

Blacksod Bay in Co Mayo. Again, I checked with the expert, and Kerry Byrnes told me it was a safe anchorage and that it was from the Blacksod weather station that the weather forecast was received to decide to go ahead with the D-Day landing in 1944. When we anchored in Blacksod it was then a desolate place, and from reports, the older hands informed us that there was nothing over there to go ashore to. So instead we decided that if we visited Killybegs for the weekend, we would have a good piss-up for I believed the residents there were extremely friendly and the women very beautiful.

When the ship was secure at her mooring, pay parade was announced and we all assembled in the focsle (the seaman's mess). The Batt arrived with the pay ledger which contained all the crew's names, excluding officers for they were paid monthly be cheque. As Coxswain, his responsibilities as well as manning the helm during manoeuvres, and while entering and leaving harbour, also involved the ship's entire paperwork and above all the compiling of the pay roll, and ensuring that everybody receives their due amount. That was why he was allocated an office and a typewriter, a prized possession on a small vessel. Anyway unknown to myself the Batt was notoriously hopeless at paperwork, and even worse at deciding who was entitled to what amount of wages, though strangely, he always managed to order enough cash for the ship's payroll, but never figured out who should get what. When I was called mine was correct. I now collected £2.29, a rise of two shillings (10p) per week since I left recruits. But as I looked around many others were examining their money with a puzzled look on their faces, and telling their friends that their wages were incorrect. Some complained that they were short of as much as £1 — nearly half their pay, and they couldn't understand why so much was missing. They declined to approach the Batt while the officer was present in case a row developed, and that they or the Batt would be at least embarrassed. So when the officer had departed after everyone aboard was paid, one by one, they questioned him about the deficiency in their pay packets. "Well" said the Batt, "You O'Reilly, how much are you short?" "£1" answered O'Reilly. "And you, Mulligan?" "The same, Chief". "What about yourself Diamond Jim?" "I'm OK, Chief". "And what about you, Kendrick?" "Ten shillings". "Oh yes now I remember", declared the Batt. "I put ye lot on a jewman's (a saving scheme), because you were spending too much money ashore". But each one of them replied that they hardly ever went out. "We wanted the money to send home to our mothers". "Look", the Batt said, "go back to work and forget about everything, your money is as safe as a house on fire with your Cox'n. You'll have it back next week, or at the very latest, in three weeks time. It's safe anyway, now, off you go". They were naturally dumbfounded, and simply couldn't answer that lot. The Batt then had the daunting task of checking back on everyone he reckoned had received too much, and then commence demanding its safe return to be re-entered into the following week's pay ledger when the same cock up would reccur again, and again during the period he was attached to the ship.

When night fell in Blacksod Bay, the entire surroundings were in total darkness. So it was evident that electricity had not reached this region. Thunder and company were again playing poker above in the focsle, and with cash now in circulation, there was an air of excitement around the messdeck. With no radios, record players, and no other entertainment facilities available, poker or ponner (pontoon) plus the yarns, some true, but mostly false I feared, for even at my young age, I found the bulk of them totally unbelievable. The stories were coming thick and fast. The first again concerned the Batt, who they said lost a torpedo from one of the motor torpedo boats during the emergency, and was still being docked a certain amount from his wages every week to pay back to the department for the original loss of the weapon. The second involved the then Director of the Service, Captain Tommy McKenna who they accused of only being trained on Tramp Steamers, and that when he entered the Marine Service, the Naval Service's predecessor, he was transferred to one of the six MTBS under the command of Lt the "Bull" Thompson, but according to them McKenna was sent ashore and ordered to report back because of seasickness and total incompetence. It was then pointed out that this was one of the reasons why McKenna was not considered to fulfil the duties of first Director of the Naval Service when it was established in 1946. Instead, the Government picked a retired Royal Naval Commander with a DSO, called Henry Joseph Alexander Saville Jerome, generally known throughout the service as "Jake". Everyone present agreed that Jake Jerome fancied himself as an Admiral of the Fleet, because every time he undertook the general inspection on the square in Haulbowline, he addressed all the officers present by their surnames in front of the rank and file who were there in force. It was, according to the crowd assembled in the focsle, a most ignorant and embarrassing display. Pints pointed out that he shouted across the parade ground at them, and that when McKenna finally took over from him, he addressed his subordinate officers in the same fashion, and that in the RN captains are ten a penny. "He may be a fucking officer", remarked Giles Donovan, "but he certainly is no gentleman". Then, inevitably the subject again returned to women and the shortage of them. O'Reilly said the women they met on the quay wall in Dublin were the best ever, and the cheapest. "But that dirty looking fecker beside you Brady wouldn't pay the dollar (five shillings). And do you know what the dirty bitch said to him when he refused to cough up the money? 'Typical Irish, big prick and no money'." "Yeah, that's right", answered the dirt bird beside me, "but I did manage to smuggle another one of them aboard and I literally had her behind the boiler". "I bet it was hot down there", shouted Maxie from the lower bunkspace, "and if you had been caught it was definitely the digger for you and maybe a trip to the Curragh hospital's isolation unit, with a dose of something that would have kept you quiet for a good while you fucker!"

I then hit the bunk, because very early the next

morning, we were sailing up to Killybegs, another very large fishing port, and I was looking forward to arriving there and looking around its charming town. The sound of our anchor cable being taken aboard suddenly woke me up, but since it was still early morning, I decided to remain where I was, because as we left Blacksod lighthouse astern, the bitch, Maev, was again standing on her head, and being tossed about like a piece of stick on the surface. One important point that I found extremely useful was that if I lay flat on my back I didn't feel seasick, and that information was to save me much hardship and distress in the future aboard this craft and her other two sisters, the *Macha* and *Cliona*. Much later that day we entered Killybegs harbour and again we anchored some way from the fishing fleets moored alongside because the harbour was too shallow to accommodate our ship. Our diesel driven motor launch was then immediately winched over the side and secured alongside to await "Wam" Murray, our captain, and the Exec, the Yank Mahony, and other officers, and then the senior NCOs, who wished to proceed ashore to contact their families by phone, or post some cash to their wives.

Mail fresh milk and bread, and a few other vital supplies were returned from that trip, along with bottles of stout and cigarettes for the duty watch carefully hidden under the boat's floorboards. The bread and milk was a very welcome treat because we were without both for the past couple of days. Paddy Kennedy had baked a batch of bread as he called it the previous day, and despite being hungry none of the crew could stomach it, and when we dumped the lot overboard it sank to the bottom so fast that the starving seagulls didn't even have time to inspect it. To colour our tea we had been using a brand of tinned milk, called Kerry full cream milk, and that was as thick as tar, and as sweet as honey, and it definitely didn't resemble milk in any respect. Although it did colour our tea, it also destroyed the tea's flavour.

That evening while attending to the duties in the NCO's mess, Rory the Chief Stoker told me that I was on the 8 to 12 watch in the diesel generator compartment, because the other guy already detailed for it was off duty due to illness. This was a bitter disappointment for me because not alone was I on the shift that night, I was also stuck aboard the following night to undertake the same duty. I was particularly unhappy to have missed the opportunity to explore this magnificent part of Donegal, of which I had heard so many excellent reports about. The only consolation was that I could sit out and relax on deck and enjoy the sunshine, admire the town and its picturesque harbour, and the fishing boats and pleasure craft, swinging at their moorings painted the colours of the rainbow. The other clear advantage in my favour was that I wouldn't be spending any of my £2.29 wages, and would, therefore, have more to spend when we hopefully would go alongside Dublin port, or shackle up to a buoy in Dun Laoghaire harbour the following weekend.

Maybe I could learn something about diesel engines and how electricity was generated while on watch. But on that subject I was again to be frustrated. When my time approached to take over from Fleming in the diesel flat, I had hoped that perhaps the engine's performance regarding its horse power, generating capacity, or even its fuel consumption per hour would be explained to me by the PO ERA, who was also on watch for the day. But I had no such luck. His simple straightforward orders to me were "Brady, you go below and sit and watch that machine. Make sure it has adequate lub oil, and if it overheats, shut it down and call me, and I'll switch over to the steam generators". Below was this monster of a machine, which I mentioned earlier, of about 450 Horse Power. The noise of it was deafening, and it was increased by the echo caused by the sound bouncing around this steel room, that was only slightly larger than the engine itself. The area stank of diesel oil and the exhaust fumes from the engine which were escaping from a fractured pipeline. The place was boiling hot from the heat being generated by the machine, and from the warm summer's evening, and the only ventilation available came through the small opening that allowed you to enter the dungeon. Therefore, my responsibility was to sit on a wooden bench covered in diesel oil surrounded by dangerous fumes, and an unbearable smell for four hours without being allowed leave the place for any purpose whatsoever, until I was relieved at midnight. Then when I was free I was unable to make a cup of tea, or have anything to eat or even a decent wash, because no hot water could be obtained due to the galley being locked, and no electric kettles aboard the ship. So I cleaned myself as best I could and went to the bunk. But since cold water will not remove the smell and fumes of diesel oil, I was forced to bury my hands under my pillow to allow me to sleep. May I add that in those days, gloves of any sort were unheard of, as were ear covers to muffle the severe sounds we encountered when we were compelled to work within the engine room, boiler rooms and the diesel generated compartment. Even rags for cleaning our hands were scarce, and that's why the ship's company smelled. Many of my colleagues suffered from hard of hearing in later years, the effects of not having their ears covered while surrounded by extremely heavy and noisy machinery on the State's ships.

The following day the topic all around the vessel was women again, and the young ones they met at a local dance. Most agreed that the young ladies were beautiful and that their accents were an added attraction. The had a special affection for the nurses whom they also met, but unfortunately they refused to elaborate and provide specific details as to their shapes or indeed if they had scored with them. The bulk of the crew, unfortunately simply headed for the local bar, got drunk and returned to the ship. A new nickname was added to the crew, because a certain seaman, sleeping in the focsle, who on returning to the ship from shore leave, usually asked his shipmates who they met, where they went and what were their backgrounds. When he was informed that they were shop assistants, factory workers, waitresses, farmer's daughters, or simply unemployed, he always boasted that he wouldn't be seen with that class of person, and that therefore he always picked and succeeded with the Bank Manager's daughter, the daughter of the region's

Garda Chief Superintendent, the County Surgeon's daughter, and very often, the Lord Mayor's only daughter. From that day forth, he was referred to as the "Great Seducer".

During parade the following morning I was ordered to report to the engine room to act as greaser, and to assist PO Courtney Murphy on the 8-12 watch, and when I entered the engine was already warming up in preparation for sea at 9am. He then instructed me in my duties to be attended to for the following four hours. They were:

(1) To frequently inspect the gauges to ensure that the pressures did not reach danger level, as indicated by the red mark printed on the gauges.
(2) To make sure that the engines big end bearings were always cool, and that plenty of oil and water was added to ensure that this was so.
(3) To oil the generators and frequently check the lubrication on the Telemoter that regulated the rudder.

Again there were no details about how anything worked, or even their horse power. Maybe they were sticking rigidly to the belief that a little knowledge can be a dangerous thing. But then I had an abundance of what Confucius said was most needed for learning, "a humble mind", and it wasn't being fed anything, except what I managed to acquire and store for the future.

We lifted and hosed down our anchor to remove the harbour's mud and put to sea, and yet again she started bobbing about like a cork and again I was dreadfully seasick, and dreaming of dry land, and let me emphasise that this was a summer's day. She was a horribly cruel bitch but life goes on and I have my responsibilities to attend to. When the engine bearings required inspection we were forced to lean into the engine and bend across a steel rail no thicker than a fountain pen. That was our only protection from actually falling under the huge pistons. As we stretched into the engine to touch their bottom ends to monitor its temperature and its lubricant content, you were in severe danger, unless you took adequate precautions that you did not do so as the ship rolled in that direction, because you could easily be thrown under the machine and crushed to death.

The most dreadful place on board was without doubt the steering flat, commonly known as the 'Black Hole of Calcutta'. It was a real nasty little place, near the stern, obviously since it was designed to move the ship's rudder. Its area was only about six feet by six feet, with a tiny hatch fitted directly above the motor to allow you inspect it. As you entered the room the smell of hot steam mixed with grease and oil dripping from the machine made me vomit at once. When you landed in the place, we only had enough room to stand and we could only barely see the motor because of the steam gushing around it. The deck head and bulk heads were dripping water continuously due to the steam condensing in the area. We simply couldn't breath for the few moments we needed to inspect everything. When we again reached the deck and fresh air again, we once more got sick over the side. So it continued hour after hour, until the task was completed. It must be stressed that the officers lived in very spartan, though more comfortable surroundings than the remainder of the crew. But they were exposed to all weathers on an open bridge, while they also undertook a four hour duty watch. A very fine gentleman, Commander Walter Reidy whom I visited years after his retirement was confined to a wheelchair with severe arthritis which was according to him, the result of being exposed to the elements on the bridges of the three corvettes with nothing for protection, except a single strip of painted canvas placed around the bridge. Walter Reidy a fine sailor, was allocated the responsibility of taking delivery of the three corvettes in turn and sailing back the *Macha* on 15.11.46, the *Maev* on 20.12.46, and Cliona on 2.3.47. The *Macha* was formally *HMS Borage K120, Maev HMS Oxlip K127*, and *Cliona HMS Belwort K114*. All flower class corvettes were as I mentioned before named after flowers, but there was definitely nothing soft or delicate about them. They had a range of 3400 miles, cruising at 9 knots. Rory McCarthy, a crew member who was detailed to accompany Walter Reidy to England to collect the *Maev*, told me that the entire crew were dispatched aboard the old *SS Kenmare* from Cork, as steerage class passengers to England along with a shipment of cattle for company, and that their only accommodation was wooden benches down aft. The Kenmare rolled like a whore during the entire night's voyage. Perhaps this was a trial run for the future aboard the corvettes?

However, as we sailed around the coast it was announced that we would be visiting Lough Swilly for the night, and that we would be anchoring with no shore leave being granted. As we entered the Lough I was informed that there were three Lough Swilly lights: Fanad, Dunree, and Buncrana, and that the oldest of these was Fanad Head, on the western shore, facing the wide open Atlantic, and that it was officially opened on St Patrick's Day 1817. When we steamed into the Lough the sheer size of its anchorage was simply breathtaking. Anchored in line were a fleet of approximately twenty Shell oil tankers of about 8,000 tons each in mothballs, due to the then slump in world oil demands. Most noticeably, was that they all looked alike, and were possibly constructed at the same shipyard from the same blueprint. Despite their numbers, and our ship moored at her anchorage, there still remained adequate space for a very large fleet of ships. Indeed, this Lough, along with Berehaven and Cobh (then Queenstown), were highly important locations for the huge fleets of warships at the Royal Navy's disposal, during the First World War. The above three ports were later to be referred to as the "Treaty Ports" and when the British Battleship Royal Oak was sunk by a German submarine at Scapa Flow, Churchill demanded that Britain must have the treaty ports back from Éire as alternative deep anchorage ports. But De Valera refused to hand them back, pointing out that this would affect our country's neutrality.

However, the following morning, I was again assigned the 8-12 watch in the engine room. When we proceeded to sea at 9am, I continued when I could to ask the self-proclaimed navigational expert Kerry Byrnes what landmarks we were passing. He pointed out Rathlin Island, the Maiden's Rock, then St John's Point in Co Down, and according to himself, she flashes her lights twice every 7.5 seconds, and what's more, there's a second Haulbowline near Carlingford Lough further down the coast. That particular light was constructed after a request from the merchants of Newry in 1817., originally, as a warning in foggy weather, a bell was rung by a machine every thirty seconds.

This patrol was then becoming very boring because for hours we neither spotted any Irish or foreign fishing vessels. But then every alarm bell on the ship went off, and panic gripped each member of the crew. When the quartermaster announced "Abandon ship!" everyone commenced running around in circles with a look of fear in their eyes, my immediate reaction was:

(1) That we had struck a mine, for I knew that over 5,000 were still unaccounted for since the war.
(2) That we had hit a submerged object, maybe an uncharted wreck or rock.
(3) That the Royal Navy had fired at us and caused terminal damage to our vessel for sailing too close to Northern Ireland territory.
(4) That the ship's hull was rotting, and I had volunteered to go to sea in a sieve.

Within minutes everybody had assembled on deck, and again, Lt the Yank Mahony, was in charge of everything and calling the shots. On spotting me he said, "You, Brady, should be in the engine room, and not on deck". "But, Sir", I replied, it's Abandon ship and since I'm not the captain, I'm not going down with her". "Do you know what life raft you're detailed for?" "No, Sir". "Well, get fecking down to the main companionway and check the detail on the board". "Is she sinking Sir?" I asked. "Just go below and check your station", he replied. As I was making my way down, the heroes from the focsle head were running around like headless chickens onto the upper deck clutching personal belongings, and tying firmly around their chests the strings of their lifejackets. McCluskey remarked that the jackets would only keep them afloat for four hours before the fish got them. I even noticed tears running down the eyes of the so-called hard men aboard. They always appear to be the first to crack! One CPO said that no matter what, he was abandoning this tub and that he would rather be a live AB than a dead CPO. So much for leadership qualities! I checked my life raft and found that I was assigned to No 2, on the port side, and on my way back up on deck I also put a lifejacket under my arm, just in case. The ship was now lying dead in the water a sitting duck, I thought for an enemy sub. As we rolled about the steam safety valve lifted on the boiler and released the pressure that had built up since the ship had stopped, thereby adding extra fear into the situation. The Yank then asked everybody individually did they know their assigned abandon ship position on deck, and when he was satisfied that they did indeed understand what lifeboat and life raft they were supposed to be in, should the vessel be in danger of sinking, he dismissed everyone, and announced that it was only an exercise. It was a case of "Fuck you, Yank Mahony!" for many days after that. In my eyes it at least separated the men from the boys. The ship then returned to her normal routine, and I finished my watch about thirty minutes later.

After dinner I decided that rather than go below into the stinking bunkspace for a nap, I would remain on deck and get some badly needed fresh air. I was also very keen to continue my knowledge of the lighthouses and landmarks as we sailed past them. This exercise also helped to release my mind from my major worry the persistent seasickness. Various crew members from seaman's division helped me with the identification of some lights when the bosun wasn't available, for they had easy access to the chart room under the bridge, which was also off limits to me, since I didn't belong to that branch and according to the officers, I didn't have any business being there. To be fair they never interfered in our responsibilities. Anyway, when we left the entrance to Carlingford Lough behind us, they explained that the Dundalk light structure was similar to the Spit Bank in Cork harbour, and was therefore easily recognisable. As we approached Drogheda, it was becoming clear from all reports that we would be either anchoring outside Dun Laoghaire during the night, or waiting until first light and then shackle to a buoy in the harbour itself. We did in fact attach ourselves to the buoy early next morning while I was asleep, after completing my 8-12 watch the previous night. The noise and excitement in the messdeck woke me up early, and it was evident that the entire crew were in jubilant mood, and the reason was that shore leave was granted from 2pm that afternoon. I was however, stuck on the 8-12 shift in the dreaded dungeon, the diesel compartment, but fortunately I was off duty after that was completed until the last launch back to the ship at midnight.

Shortly after dinner was served in the messes there was a rush for the washhouse, and just like in the billets the thought of going ashore resulted in the rush for the 'Old Spice Aftershave', the razors and as much hot water from the galley as possible, plus of course the inevitable current love songs of Nat King Cole, Jo Stafford, and Eddie Fisher. They were the first songs that I heard since joining this craft, and that was a definite sign that the rank and file were really happy. Together, we all changed into our civvies and fell in on deck for checking out by the quartermaster whose job it was to ensure that all had returned by twelve that night because we were steaming again possibly to Rosslare the next morning at 9am. As we made our way onto the pier I was surprised at the number of very expensive private yachts moored in this magnificent harbour. Most were Irish but a large number were British, and a few were American. The largest vessel at anchor was a motor vessel owned by the Guinness brewing company. All were perfectly maintained and glittering in the gorgeous summer afternoon.

When we disembarked as was usually the case, the group split up into smaller sections and then went their separate ways. I headed for the nearest newsagents and purchased a birthday card for Ann in Cobh, and immediately posted it in the GPO opposite the Mail Boat's pier, and then I decided to buy her a present of a gold cross and chain (well, it looked gold), in a jeweller's shop in George's Street. Then I jumped onto the bus for Dublin, and when it reached its terminus, I rushed over to McBirneys on Aston Quay and caught the 79, which would leave me outside my mother's door. When she opened the door and saw me she nearly had a stroke, because since I was home during the afternoon she assumed that I had been either kicked out of the service, or more likely deserted. Her first words were "I hope the police won't be looking for you because I'm not going to be made a show of up here, with that crowd of busy bodies living around here watching everything that's going on. And where's that lovely suit and overcoat that I bought you from Mary down in the Iveagh market before you went into that Navy place?" "I thought that I explained that to you mother in my letter. Can you not remember that I told you a young chap joined up in rags, and that I felt sorry for him, and gave them to him to wear ashore". "Nobody ever gave us anything. I always had to work for everything that I ever got", and so she went on. Then she said "Are they feeding you on them ships, because you look half starved to me. Are you getting any fresh air, and the smell of you, there's a smell of grease and oil off you". If I gave the wrong answers to her things could get real difficult for me because she would think nothing of going to a TD or even a barrister and complaining about how her son was being treated, and then make life difficult for me with the top brass in GHQ or in Haulbowline. So I told here that conditions on the ship couldn't be better. We all had our own cabins with hot and cold running water. We had a choice of meals, and we could eat any time day or night, and that when the weather was bad, we would rush to the nearest port for shelter. "If I catch you lying Jim Brady, I'll break your effin face. Now go in there and make us a cup of tea. Where's the pound for the jewman towards the loan I got you from him to buy that lovely suit you're wearing?"

I turned on the Bush radio and listened to a soccer match until the other eight arrived back for their tea, and then I decided to head for the pictures in Inchicore to see a western, and when that finished, I returned to Dun Laoghaire, and only just caught the midnight boat back to the Maev which was at this stage, lit up like a Christmas tree. The boat's crew revealed to us that the officers in the wardroom were entertaining women whom they had met ashore, and according to the lads they were all pissed drunk. Tierney said that he wasn't allowed to bring his own brother aboard, while alongside Dublin on an earlier patrol. So much for equality! Below most of the crew were asleep, while the remainder were again talking about the birds they saw and met in the pubs and dance halls in Dublin. I was beginning to think that they had women on the brain. Anyway, at exactly 9am the next morning, McCluskey, Pints and a few more rowed around in the seaboat to unshackle our anchor cable from the buoy, and when that was completed the boat was hoisted aboard by the derricks, and then we proceeded very slowly away from the harbour to ensure that we did not disturb the luxury yachts with our wash for fear of complaints or claims for damages against the Department of Defence. As we passed Wicklow Head, I said to myself, "wouldn't it be beautiful lying on the Silver Strand ashore with Ann in her bathing suit, along with a bucket full of ice cold Carlsberg?"

The bloody ship kept reminding me of what a bitch she was. The Maev was still rolling her guts out, and again this was a glorious summer's day. Monsarrat, in the book, 'The Cruel Sea', says that they would roll on wet grass. From my experience of them so far they roll alongside, at anchor, shackled to a buoy, in the most sheltered of harbours, and at sea even when it's flat calm. So, it's clearly a design fault. I was detailed for the 12-4 watch this time, in the boiler room with Tierney the senior rating to instruct me. At that stage he knew only a little more than I, but he instructed me in the knowledge of the job he had acquired through trial and error. Roughly this is what he told me. The two boilers are fire tube types and each has a steam pressure capacity of 225 lbs per square inch, but that we in the stokehold always keep the pressure at 220 PSI for safety reasons, and if it goes above 225 PSI, the safety valve lifts and she blows off the steam pressure. The fuel oil is heated to 180 degrees Fahrenheit, before its pumped into the furnaces through a sprayer that has large or small tips fitted to them, depending on the amount of steam that's required for the various speeds of the ship. Each boiler had a Howden forced draught system connected to them for efficient combustion. He then demonstrated the method of checking the level of water in the boilers, by examining their gauge glasses, and then explained the mechanism of the feed pump that pumped water into the boilers, as required. Finally, if more speed is called for urgently, we must, without delay, operate the fuel pumps to their full capacity. Otherwise the steam pressure would drop and the ship would be soon stopped dead in her tracks. "Then", he said, "For God's sake, don't make black smoke, because Cody, during his shift the other night blackened the Captain, the Yank and a few others on the bridge. And guess what the mad fucker told them when he was sent for to explain 'what fucking colour do you lot want for £2.29!' He was charged with gross insubordination". When we completed our duty without incident we were filthy from the effects of the heavy black crude oil, and like everyone else the only means we had of removing that type of substance was with the stinking diesel oil, the fumes of which were also extremely difficult to remove.

After tea we entered the wide anchorage of Rosslare Harbour, and from where we were moored, the locality then looked desolate and bare, and there was no shore leave which was very disappointing to the number of Wexford men whom we had serving aboard. The included the Whites, Walshes, Kehoes and Roches. But the following morning, they were on the after deck explaining the Tuskar Rock, a large white tower, seven miles out from the coast. I shall return to that most famous chunk of rock later on. Then they pointed out the Conningbeg light vessel. Later on, down the east coast, Kerry Byrnes spotted Hook Head, at the entrance to Waterford; Dunmore East, Helvic Head, and Ballycotton, the home of the famous lifeboat. Then, thank heavens, we entered Cork harbour again after passing Roches Point on our starboard side. As we re-entered our home port, I noticed almost directly opposite Roches Point, the old fort of Templebreedy, and further inside the harbour, again on our port side, Camden Fort, and further, on our starboard side, Fort Carlisle. In the centre with her battery of 6 inch guns facing south, Spike Island, and Fort Mitchel. As we turned ninety degrees to port at the Spit lighthouse, I observed another gun emplacement below the former British Army compound at the Holy Grounds. The above formed part of the defence for the British Headquarters of the South Irish Coastal defence system.

Farewell to Ann

Immediately after tying up at the oil wharf, Chief McCarthy ordered me to commence pumping fresh water aboard, while he undertook the delicate task of directing the refuelling of the heavy crude oil onto the ship. This operation was precisely controlled to enable each fuel tank aboard to receive the exact amount as the others. This ensured that all tanks, which were fitted on the port and starboard sides were level, and therefore, the ship was on an even keel. O'Meara then delivered food and supplied for the ship's company, because we were on standby duty in case we were called out in an emergency. I then contacted Ann by phone in Cork, and we arranged to meet at the usual place at 7.30 that evening, and since I was very aware that myself and the remainder of the crew smelled of dirt, grease, oil, and whatever else, I decided to visit the base's canteen and purchase a large bar of lux soap, a bottle of their best shampoo, and with my old spice aftershave, I headed for the shower room in the main billet. I remained under the shower for nearly thirty minutes, with the temperature regulated to a level as high as I could bear, and used almost half of the bar of soap, and shampooed my hair thoroughly a few times,until I was satisfied that I no longer smelled like a caged animal in a zoo. I then returned to the *Maev*, and along with about half the crew, changed into our civvies, and ran for the ten past seven DOD launch, the John Adams, and when we reached our pier at Cobh, I headed straight across to the Commodore, and I was absolutely delighted to spot her there waiting patiently, and looking gorgeous in her light summer dress, her hair cut short, and her suntanned arms, neck and face, which gave her a very sexy female appearance. Her first question was, "why didn't you phone me from around the coast?" When I tried to explain that I was only once ashore, in Dublin, she then said, "you're stinking of diesel oil, and why don't you wash yourself when you come over here to meet me?", and then, "where's my birthday present you promised me?" When I produced the cross and chain, which was still wrapped in the box with the jeweller's name printed on it, she declared that it was only rolled gold, and not 18 carat gold as I stated. I reckoned it was going to be an extremely difficult evening, and from her mannerisms, it was evident that she had something on her mind, and therefore, had plotted some plan of action. I was proved right and it didn't take her too long to show her cards. Automatically, we again headed to the Well House, which was as usual packed to the rafters with young navy chaps serving themselves and the proprietor, who was sitting with a group around a large table, was almost paralysed from the excessive consumption of alcohol.

Ann and myself settled for ice cold lager, while she smoked 'Craven A' cigarettes from her stainless steel cigarette case, covered in crocodile skin. After a couple of hours and several drinks later, the conversation finally drifted towards the Navy, the ships and their long patrols, and curiously she again asked me did I intend signing on and making a career out of it. I again repeated that I had no intentions of staying down there due to the conditions aboard ship, the bullshit, rotten food, dangerous ships, and lack of career prospects.

"So then you won't be staying in Cobh?" "Definitely not" I replied, "because when my time is up, I'm heading straight back to Dublin or London". "Well, I'm not moving from my home town, and that's it". "I never asked you to, Ann", I replied. She then showed her cards, when she said that she attended a dance two nights earlier, and met according to her, a lovely fellow from Cork City, who was in Cobh for a wedding, and that he had asked her out. "And did you accept?" "No not then, but I might because I told him where I work". The set-up was therefore obvious to me. She wanted a long-term relationship with me, provided I gave an assurance that I would sign on for a further term in the service. That much was clear from the various stories and reports that I had heard across in Haulbowline, concerning the Cobh girls. The bottom line was they wanted security, and were willing to continue with you provided you had a steady job. Well, that makes good sense, and who's to blame them? I left her home and without returning to the subject, we both knew the situation. I then caught the boat back to the base and returned to my ship, and the 4-8 watch below watching the bloody diesel generator. We never contacted one another again, and I only spotted her once years later, in Scotts Square, Cobh. She looked more beautiful than ever, and clearly very happy with a little boy and girl, along with her husband, a CPO in uniform. Well at least I thought, she married a navy chap. Then I felt a little disappointed that it wasn't me.

At 9am sharp on Monday morning it was back again to sea for another three weeks of boring patrolling around the coast. This time the only difference to the previous trip, was that we visited several different ports, including Bantry Bay and Valentia. We also passed Kerry Head and Loop Head, and made our own way up the Shannon, to Foynes. Our next duty brought us around the Aran Islands, and then we anchored in Galway Bay for that night. The following visit was to Clew Bay where we rested on another occasion. We also revisited the harbours that I referred to during our last patrol. That monotonous routine continued on the *Maev* for the next fourteen months during which time, I was advanced to AB First Class, and shortly afterwards transferred to the *Cliona* where, thankfully, I again teamed up with my real pals from recruits days, Stretch, Doyler, Muxer, Hume, Hector, and Jim Roche. The ship was exactly the same, except that the aft boiler's starboard furnace was twisted and had moved away from its fixtures. This highly dangerous fault was clearly visible to the naked eye through the inspection opening from the boiler room. A few wise stokers, notably Georgie refused to fire that furnace and suffered the severest of consequences thereafter.

I was shocked and saddened when I inspected the awful conditions in which my mates were existing. They were filthy and obviously ill-nourished, and very tired looking and ill at ease. I wondered why until I visited the messdeck for my first meal, and there I was also shocked to find my friends and their comrades drinking their tea out of lamp shades, and cutting up their meals with screw drivers. I asked them why they had been living like pigs on a state ship, and not complaining. They said that they did complain to the officers several times, but they said that the civil service would not replace the cutlery or delph that was lost overboard or broken in rough weather. "This is a ridiculous situation" I told them. "We are not convicted criminals, but volunteers who decided to serve the state on state ships, and we are treated like dirt". But despite the hardship filthy living and working conditions, she was a happy ship, because there was a happy crew aboard her. My new exec was the now very unpredictable Hock, who insisted on falling the crew in on the upper deck every morning before 8am, for inspection in all weathers, and he also grew into a habit of charging everyone he notice with even their shoelaces untied and bringing them before the captain. My new boss in the engine room was CPO Con McCarthy whose favourite tools for the most delicate of repairs were the seven pound sledge hammer, and the four foot steel pinch bar. If something didn't work after the initial attempt, Con simply shouted out "Bring me the seven pounder", and then used a lot of not so gentle persuasion, and to our surprise, that crude method frequently worked.

We continued tramping around the coastline month after month, with not the slightest chance of a foreign cruise. That dreaded routine was only broken by a visit to a decent port, such as Waterford, Limerick, Galway, or Dublin, and sometimes by the arrest of a foreign fishing vessel, usually a Frenchman, or Spaniard, for illegally fishing within our territorial seas, and then escorted to the nearest harbour and handed over to the local Gardaí to prepare court proceedings against them.

On The Curragh Plains

After approximately twelve months of that gloomy patrol work, the Cox'n Brian McLarnan asked me to go to his office, and when he heard me making my way towards him, he ordered me to stop whistling because he said "it's unlucky to whistle aboard ship". It is something to do with whistling for wind. Anyway, he asked me did I want to be considered for an NCO's course. I was of course totally surprised, and I somehow managed to stutter out "Yes, Cox'n", not being fully sure if he actually meant it. But then he added "send Lynch, Doyle, and Power down to me right away". "Yes, Cox'n", I said. I was astonished. Myself, Stretch, Doyler, Hector and fourteen others including Tit Murtagh from various sections of the navy were about to commence the 38th potential NCO's course in the Curragh Camp, and a three month holiday break from the ships was about to start. What, we wondered would the soldiers in their green uniforms think of us, and we of them?

We travelled by train from Cobh to Sallins, in Kildare, and then we were brought from there by Army lorry to the Curragh. When we arrived we were all assembled on the square for counting and checking of names, and then the officer in charge of the course, Captain Bowles, introduced us to his staff, first his assistant officers, Captain O'Sullivan, Lt Grennan and Lt McKevitt. Then our instructors, C/S Daly, Sgts

Ambrose, Sexton, Shannon, Murray, Conneely, McKearney, Lloyd and Kearney. While everyone stood to attention, Capt Bowles pointed out that we were chosen for this course because we had shown some leadership qualities, and that it was his, and his staff's responsibility to improve on those qualities. Then he added, "your instruction starts tomorrow morning and I will not tolerate troublemakers of any sort. You are the future leaders, and your example is extremely important within the defence forces, and I hope that we can work together with our comrades from the Naval Service. Now dismiss the men C/S Daly". "Brood! Shas eeg Arash!" shouted C/S Daly. "I am your senior NCO", said Daly, and if any of you lot cross me or refuse my instructions, you'll be on the first truck out of this place. This course is all about discipline, and that's what I want from you because without discipline in the ranks, the defence forces fail to function properly". Then he shouted "Brood Aire! Shass eeg Arash! Leag Amac!" "Sgt Ambrose, escort the navy men to their billet".

We were marched to a nearby quarters that was to our delight, completely separated from the soldiers in our class. The place was clean and comfortable, and when Sgt Ambrose said to us that we knew what to wear on parade the following day it was evident to us that the army was unfamiliar with our uniform. We then decided to turn this to our advantage. Paddy Drohan suggested that if we all attended parade ground obligations, class room lectures, manoeuvres, and drills of all sorts dressed the same the soldiers would never tell whether we were dressed properly or improperly. That masterstroke worked completely to our advantage, because depending on the weather or our humour, we dressed as we pleased, but always clean and tidy for we were never going to disgrace ourselves in any way within an army compound.

The course itself was no more difficult than the recruit's training that we endured with Ferriter It consisted of the usual foot and arms drill on the square, class room instruction, voice control and projection under Capt O'Sullivan, plus leadership lectures, map reading, and the maintenance of weapons. We undertook route marches, war games on the Curragh plains, all night manoeuvres that included marching through deep rivers with full packs and fully armed, in the Glen of Immal, Co Wicklow. Overall, we considered it a rest and a holiday, and the bonus was that 1959 turned out to be a glorious summer, and every morning before training we were ordered to attend the swimming pool which we did without too much persuasion. We were also excused duties during our entire stay since we were undergoing training, and every weekend was free which enabled us to visit our parents, if we so wished. We managed to avoid wearing our No 1 uniform until the passing out parade when we decided to include our white belt and leggings and paid great attention to the brasswork on the belt, and cap-badge. With the Commanding Officer of the barracks Colonel McCormack taking the salute, we along with the Curragh Band felt and looked immaculate and confident. Need I add that we all passed out with flying colours!

I Rejoin the Flotilla

When I returned to Haulbowline, I was a leading stoker First Class, and without any congratulations or even a comment about the course, I was dispatched to join the Macha as a leading hand in the engine room and boiler room, and since I now knew more about soldering, but very little more than those under me on the ship, I decided to acquire a few books that were available in the naval base library. They were The Machinery Handbook BR77, Patrol Service Handbook BR112, Notes on Damage Control, NC Ships, Fire Fighting Manual SFFM, Accountancy and Administration Instructions A7A1, Ships Drawings S Ships Standing Orders SSO. They gave me an idea of pumping and flooding of watertight compartments, calculating of fuel consumption at sea and in harbours, and the supervising of cleaning and working in fuel compartments; feed water treatment; fire fighting and damage control; heat and steam; force energy work and power; corvettes main and auxiliary machinery; internal combustion engines; ventilation of fuel tanks; the layout of portable suction pumps; the maintenance of the windless and steering gear; the organisation of naval stores and repair parties, and the force and work of a four stroke engine. When I read and understood some of that lot, I then went to the Cork County library and took out on loan Steam Boilers by William H Fowler, published by the Scientific publishing company; Modern Methods of Water Purification by John Don and John Chisholm, published by Edward Arnold; and Marine Engines and Boilers: Their Design and Construction, by Bauer and Robinson, published by Crosby Lockwood. I reckoned that even if I digested a section of what was contained in the above books, I would have the edge over the others in my branch aboard ship. It was a huge advantage knowing how to treat boiler water, how the engine and boilers performed, how to shore up watertight compartments if they were damaged, and even how a four stroke engine worked. But the repair and maintenance of the ship's machinery parts was strictly off limits to me because I was not a tradesman (an engine room artificer). However, I undertook my duties aboard the Macha during the following year to the best of my ability. Finally, I along with George Carr was transferred back to the *Cliona* where the damaged furnace had even further deteriorated, and according to the staff operating the boiler room, it had not even been inspected. I was then also informed that one of the furnaces in the *Maev's* boilers had split wide open and allowed the steam to enter the furnace. The ship was forced to return to port under much less power. So it was quite obvious to me that the navy's ships were becoming highly dangerous to sail on, and I was therefore not sorry that my commitment to the service was almost completed.

I was also told that the PO Cook Paddy Kennedy, the man who used to stir the tea with the nearest brush handle, had decided to retire, and on his last trip, he made a special meal for the entire crew, including rice pudding with raisins added, and a little strawberry jam as an extra attraction. As a further celebration treat for the officers, because he hated all officers, whom he blamed for all his misfortunes, he added the cockroaches that lived in their thousands aboard ship, especially in the food lockers. He disguised the dreaded insects by cutting them up, and then inserting them into the raisins. The unfortunate officers never knew the difference, neither did their waiters, who served them in their wardroom. Paddy and his wife later opened a very successful restaurant in Cobh, and refused to serve officers including the Yank Mahony who was a decent chap and had absolutely nothing to do with Paddy's position.

I finally left the *Cliona* which in my estimation was a danger to shipping, and then the service, in 1962, with an exemplary discharge from the naval base's Commanding Officer. After a good session in the base NCOs mess, with the Batt, Kerry Byrnes, Pongo, Paddles, the Camel Driver, Gene O'Shea, Nick Kennedy, Tit Murtagh and CPO Keaney, another great friend, along with Stretch and company, I said my lengthy goodbyes to all my smashing mates who stuck together through thick and thin, and through the dirt and filthy living conditions on disgraceful ships. As I made my way through the gate at the guard room, with tears in my eyes, for I was sad to leave very many friends behind, a group of four very young officer cadets marched past me, and as I turned to admire them, I asked the guard commander who they were. "The senior midshipman out in front is John Kavanagh, and the other three are Charles O'Donnell, Peadar McElhenny and Owen McNamara", he replied. "Well", I said, the navy's future appears to be in safe hands because those four lads certainly look very bright indeed". I am delighted to report that today the service's commodore and flag officer commanding the entire service is John Kavanagh. The commanding officer of Haulbowline is Captain PJA McElhinny and Charles O'Donnell and Owen McNamara are both commanders and hold senior appointments within the service.

The Navy's Darkest Period

After my discharge I tried to keep in touch with the service to which I owed so much, while working and living in London. Through a Cork friend staying in the same accommodation as myself, I frequently read the Cork Weekly Examiner, and when he handed me the edition of 31 May 1962, I almost died of shock, because the headline read "Fire Drama on Corvette". The subheading read "Valiant Crew Saves Ship — three injured". A third heading said "Depth Charge Fractures Oil Feed Pipes". The article went on to report that the ship suffered from severe concussion after firing depth charges from the stern, and the aftershock caused the fuel supply lines in the No 1 boiler room to fracture and cause a huge fire.

This drama occurred during the ship's annual exercise when journalists from several national newspapers were normally aboard to witness the vessel firing their guns at targets being towed by the launch John Adams. Then the two depth charge throwers on both sides of the ship, and the rails on the stern discharged patterns of depth charges that are set to explode at various depths. If a charge is set to explode at a shallow depth of say, two hundred feet, the ship must be travelling at high speed to clear the area, otherwise, her stern, instead of the enemy's ship would be blown off. But if the charge is set for a much deeper depth of about 700 feet, the vessel need not be clearing the area too fast, simply because the device would not have reached its intended depth until they had well cleared the danger zone. It was never proved what caused the Cliona to be almost lost with certain death to some of her crew. Nobody knows the exact cause, but it was possibly:

(1) A faulty depth charge.
(2) Human error on the crew attending to the depth charge rails on the after deck.
(3) A breakdown in communications between the officers on the bridge who ordered the depth

> settings to be set on the charges before discharging the anti-submarine explosives over the side and stern of the vessel.

The most likely cause was that a shallow depth was set instead of a much deeper setting, and they had not completely left the locality of the blast. Whatever the cause, the Navy's ship that I had only left five months previously, was almost lost, but for the brave action of one particular stoker Willie Mynes, who suffered severe burns while closing down the valves on a fuel tank that was feeding a raging fire which was engulfing the ship. The remainder of the firefighters aboard the ship, under the guidance, determination and bravery of the ship's exec, the Yank Mahony, brought the fire under control, and ordered the ship's lifeboats and carley floats to be on stand by in case the order for abandon ship was given by the Captain, Lt-Cmdr Harry Henry. The fire-damaged boiler room was closed down and the other one restarted, and the ship returned to Cork harbour under her own steam. When she reached her base the burned personnel were immediately rushed to the military hospital in Cork. A high degree of bravery and professionalism was shown that day, but two cowards did in fact leave the ship in a boat without the order being given by the captain. A few well deserved medals should have been issued after that event, or at the very least rapid promotion for the key players, because they definitely saved lives and most probably, the *LE Cliona*.

Later investigations did reveal that the boiler room fittings where the fire started were rotting, and therefore could never have survived the shock of an explosion close by. So, I felt justified that my conjecture about the ageing corvettes was correct, that they should be scrapped forthwith, but, unfortunately, nobody listened to me. More evidence that the ships were useless was revealed when the Aer Lingus Viscount plane crashed on Sunday morning, 24th March 1968, near the Tuskar Rock lighthouse off the Wexford coastline. The 'St Phelim' was lost with sixty one persons on board. The mystery of the air disaster has never been definitely solved, but it is widely believed that a British Naval or Army missile of some sort, which was being tested in the vicinity, went off course and out of control, and then struck the tail of the passenger plane, putting her into a fatal spin. However, the Irish Navy were nowhere to be seen. So, the British Navy's Frigate *HMS Pentelope*, and *HMS Hardy*, and a civilian manned naval vessel Invermoriston, promptly took control of the entire operation, searching for possible survivors and for wreckage.

The *Cliona* and *Maev* were tied up in Haulbowline. The *Cliona* was on leave period, and *Maev* was out of commission because no spare parts were now available to repair her. The *Macha* then was the only ship available to patrol our 2000 mile coastline, and she was at anchor in Killybegs Co Donegal, and the most unforgivable aspect of our Navy's involvement was that the *Macha* did not arrive as the crash scene until the following Tuesday morning, two days after the event. In the meantime, the front page of *The Irish Times* of that same morning, Tuesday, 26th March 1968, showed the RNs Frigate *HMS Hardy* landing nine bodies at Rosslare, and reported that the Hardy, under the command of Lt-Cmdr James Lord RN had also recovered large sections of the main undercharge of the Viscount, which was later removed from the Hardy by crane while tied up alongside the pier in Rosslare. So it was clearly an entire Royal Naval Exercise conducted within our territorial waters, and then using our port of Rosslare, while our navy were moored in Haulbowline and anchored in Killybegs. The *Cliona* finally arrived off Wexford several days later by which time the RN also had stationed in the search zone the mine sweepers *HMS Shoulton* and *HMS Clabreston*, plus a salvage Vessel the *Uplifter* from Milford Haven. She was later joined by the Reclaim A diving and rescue vessel that was dispatched from Plymouth. The Royal Navy remained at the crash site until it was abandoned due to bad weather the following October, when fifty six per cent of the wreckage was recovered with the help of some local trawlers. During diving operations, the

The minesweeper "Grainne" with an Air Corps alloutte helicopter.
Photograph taken from the Deirdre.

L.E. Aoife.

The Ferdia, a trawler leased to the Navy to patrol our coastline.

L.E. Setanta, originally the Irish Lights ship Isolda built at Liffey Dockyard, Dublin in 1953.

The Aisling encounters a southerly summer gale outside Cork harbour.

L.E. Eithne at high speed.

Treasured Cork & Cobh cinema tickets to remind me of Ann, my first love.

Ciara taken from Orla during exercises.

Ciara passing Cobh.

The L.E. Niamh.
Photo: Able-Seaman David Jones, Naval Service.

The Niamh under construction in 2001 at the Appledore Shipyard in Devon, England. *Photo: The Irish Times.*

Dr. John DeCourcy Ireland, the maritime historian right; and the author left, being interviewed by Barney Yourell for his Maritime Radio Programme following a ceremony in Cathal Brugha Military Barracks, Dublin on 18.11.2001.

A Delta Rigid Inflatable Boat. (RIB). *Photo: Chief Petty Officer G. T. Whitston.*

The L.E. Róisín. *Photo: Able-Seaman David Jones, Naval Service.*

The Eithne about to anchor in New York Harbour during her visit for the re-dedication of the Statue of Liberty in 1986 with the now infamous Twin Towers in the background. Able-Seaman, now Petty Officer; Michael Kelly left; Ensign, now Lt-Commander Peter Toomey centre; Able-Seaman Matt Byrne right. *Photograph: Chief Petty Officer G. T. Whitston.*

Dublin Adopts Ship

Dublin Corporation have officially adopted the Naval Vessel, L.E. Róisín. This is the first ship to be adopted by Dublin City. Dublin City has a long maritime history and is the location of Ireland's busiest port. 'After the initial adoption ceremony, a bond is established' said the Lord Mayor Alderman Maurice Ahern. The L.E. Róisín, a state-of-the-art off shore patrol vessel was comissioned last December and built in North Devon, England.

She was named by Mary Smith, wife of Michael Smith TD, Minister for Defence, on the 9th September last year. The ship is of steel construction, is 79 metres in length, 14 metres wide and has a gross tonnage of 1500 tonnes. Alderman Ahern added 'The citizens of Dublin will look upon the L.E. Róisín as their own ship. When the Ciy requires a Naval Vessel for ceremonial purposes, or for a marine based event, then its own ship L.E. Róisín will, where possible be used.' Lt. Commander Brian Heavers of the L.E. Róisín said that the Commanding Officer and Ships Company of the L.E. Róisín look forward to a long association with the citizens of the Dublin. In Irish poetry Róisín or Róisín Dubh is usually portrayed as an allegory for Ireland. Historically she was probably one of the daughters of Red Hugh O'Neill, Earl of Tyrone in the late 16th century.

The Róisín 'camouflaged' and published by Dublin Extra, a Life Times publication on 5.9.2000

The Niamh with the Ciara left, fighting a fire aboard the fishing trawler Fiona Patricia, eighteen miles off the Cork Coast in September 2001. *Photo: Irish Coastguard.*

Reclaim took part in ninety one dives in depths of 250 feet of water over a period of twenty six days during that summer, which they later claimed was the most difficult and dangerous underwater operation ever undertaken by the Royal Navy. Our two operational ships only showed a token presence from time to time during that extremely vital period.

Further evidence that they were almost useless was that during that same year, all three corvettes were stripped of their standard armament. Removed were their two-pounder Pom-Pom gun, plus the two 20 MM Oerlikon anti aircraft guns. Their Hedgehog anti-submarine system and the four depth charge throwers and rails and only the updated first world war four inch gun remained on their bows. So not alone were they no longer regarded as naval vessels they were also unseaworthy and a danger to their young crews aboard them. Therefore, I felt that they must be decommissioned and scrapped without delay. I felt so strong for their safety of my friends and former colleagues that I presented my case for the removal of the ships to the nation through the columns of our national newspapers, and I also wrote to certain people in authority, who possessed a little influence, to press forward the important message that we urgently required replacement vessels for the existing scrap that we had patrolling our seas. Still nobody listened and nothing was done, as the navy drifted into rapid decline.

In December that year, the *Macha* was decommissioned and cannibalised for usable spare parts to help towards keeping the other two operational. But eight months later, the *Cliona* was taken out of service because she too was falling apart, and unsafe. I continued presenting the case for ships for the navy, pointing out that as an island nation, we must have adequate protection around our 2000 mile coastline against the smuggling of arms and ammunition and wholesale plundering of our extremely valuable fish stocks by huge foreign fishing fleets complete with factory ships for processing the catches. I was simply laughed at and ignored when I also stressed that we then possessed a most modern and fully equipped shipyard, the Verolme Dockyard in Rushbrooke, only a mile from Haulbowline with a highly skilled workforce, plus the Irish steel mills beside the naval base to produce the raw material needed to construct new ships. But the following year, the Maev was also decommissioned and then without delay, all three were quickly towed away to the nearest junkyard. Then our navy entered the record books as being the only navy in the world with no ships and it was also the laughing stock of the world. It was in such a pitiful state that to provide it with some form of seagoing capability, the Department of Fisheries research vessel the CU Feasa, which was only 80 feet long and with a gross weight of only 93 tonnes was pressed into service. What a disgraceful situation! Here was a Naval Service with an unarmed punt acting as a patrol vessel to police an entire coastline with one naval officer aboard armed with a pistol. It was a shame and those responsible should never be forgiven or forgotten.

A New Beginning

Finally, in December 1970, the government was forced to act to supply the service with some type of equipment. Therefore, they reluctantly purchased from Britain three Ton class coastal minesweepers which were fully equipped down to cups and saucers, plus a huge amount of spares, for the bargain price of £640,000, thereby rescuing the naval service from total extinction. They were *HMS Oulston, HMS Alverton* and *HMS Blaxton*. The Oulston was in mothballs and in almost mint condition when she was inspected at her moorings in Hythe Southampton. She was sailed back by an Irish crew, and renamed the *LE Grainne*. The *Alverton* and *Blaxton* were handed over to our personnel in Gibraltar and then renamed *LE Banba* and *LE Fola* and sailed for home on 20th March 1971, when they encountered heavy weather, which forced them into dry dock in Lisbon for emergency repairs. Finally on the 29th March, they reached Haulbowline. Evidently, they were never designed for heavy weather, being only 153 feet in length, with a displacement of just 360 tons and a fuel capacity of 47 tons. Their hulls were of aluminium with a mahogany planking, the superstructure also being of aluminium to reduce the magnetic field while mine-sweeping. The accommodation and general living conditions within the messes aboard the sweepers was luxurious compared to the antiquated corvettes and they were powered by twin mireless diesel engines, generation 3000 HP. Their armament was also up-to-date with a power operated Bofer along with twin 20 mm Oerlikon guns.

The service also urgently required vessels capable of operating offshore in all weathers, so in February 1971, a contract was signed with the Verolme Cork dockyard to design and construct such a ship. Things were at last beginning to move. Then in August of the same year the keel was laid and on December 29th, the ship was launched and named the *LE Deirdre*, P20. The vessel was fully fitted out by May of the following year, and then handed over to the navy at a cost of £1,000,000. The service was delighted with their first ever custom built ship, because all previous craft had been purchased second hand from Britain's Royal Navy. The *Deirdre*'s dimensions are very similar to the corvettes. Her length is 205.5 feet, beam 34.5 feet, draft 15 feet and her displacement is 974 tons. Her design and crew accommodation and catering facilities were of the highest standards and were many generations ahead of the corvettes. The stabilisers are gyro controlled to reduce rolling to the absolute minimum, which also greatly controls the seagoing capabilities of the vessel. The Deirdre's only serious design problem was that she was not constructed as a naval vessel and therefore did not possess watertight compartments throughout the vessel. Although the navy now operated three coastal minesweepers and one offshore ship, but the arrest of the *MV Claudia* near Helvic Head, Co Waterford, in March 1973, loaded with five tons of arms and ammunition, bound for the IRA by the Deirdre, Fola and Grainne, proved that an effective coastal patrol was vitally important for our country.

Since the evidence was now perfectly clear, the government ordered a second Deirdre type vessel in December 1975, but unfortunately, her keel was not laid until February 1977 and she did not become fully operational until January 1978, as the *LE Emer P21*. She incorporated some very important modifications:

(1) Her watertight capabilities were vastly improved.
(2) The length of the vessel was increased.
(3) Her crew's accommodation was altered to decrease vibration and noise from the main engine.
(4) The *Emer*'s displacement was increased to 1019.59 tons.

In the meantime, the EEC Fisheries ministers decided to introduce a 200 mile exclusive economy zone to operate from the 1st January 1977. So the navy was given the responsibility of policing an area of 132,000 square miles of sea, or an area four times the size of Ireland. By this time the service had taken delivery of an ex-Irish lighthouse ship, the *SS Isolda*, and renamed it the *LE Setanta*. No purchase price was ever revealed for this craft, but it was the opinion of very many that at the time of purchase, the *Isolda* built at the Liffey dockyard in Dublin in 1953 was almost worn out and in many respects unsuitable as a naval patrol ship. Another near fatal blunder was the leasing for an undisclosed price of a Danish fishing vessel, the Helen Basse for a twelve month period from January 1977 and commissioned as the *LE Ferdia*. This was a panic reaction to the commencement of the new exclusive EEC fishing limits, and was a disastrous decision.

With fifty per cent of the cost now being funded by Brussels, a third Deirdre class was launched at the Verolme yard on 25 May 1979 and commissioned into the service on 29 November 1979 as the *LE Aoife P22*. The fourth and final Deirdre type ship was launched on 27 September 1979 and commissioned as the *Aisling* P23 on 21 May 1980. All four remain fully operational and in reasonably good condition, despite severe wear and tear in extreme weathers patrolling the 132,000 square miles of EC waters. To greatly increase the service's capabilities and effectiveness, policing such a huge area, it was decided in 1982 to construct two patrol vessels, with twice the tonnage of the *Deirdre* class and be equipped to carry helicopters. The helicopters would be flown by pilots from the Air Corps with comprehensive facilities, including accommodation for crew and technical staff, plus workshops, and refuelling services aboard. Again, the EEC funded half the £30,000,000 towards the building of the two P31 type ships and the first keel was laid in December 1982. During her construction, the Verolme dockyard encountered serious industrial and financial problems, and then the government announced that after that ship was finished, the yard would close down completely and all workers would be made redundant. So, the cost of that ship finally amounted to £28,000,000 because of delays, due to vital parts being fitted wrongly quite intentionally to prolong the building of the ship. The P31 class patrol vessel, the *LE Eithne* was finally finished and delivered to the Navy in December 1984.

She broke down on her maiden voyage from Rushbrooke to Haulbowline when the assistance of a tug was immediately required to tow her to Haulbowline. The *Eithne* is a magnificent ship in every respect, and is designed to carry two helicopters, one in the hanger, and another on the helicopter landing platform on the after deck. I have inspected Eithne perhaps one hundred and fifty times over the eleven year period since her construction, and I have never observed a helicopter aboard her, despite the fact that she was specifically designed and constructed at a vast cost to operate with and carry them. The pathetic reason for this farce is that the Air Corps refuse to serve aboard the ship, and simply only carry out exercises involving taking off and landing on the deck of the Eithne, then returning to their land base, and home for the evening, while the ship is allowed to proceed with her three weeks operational patrol alone. That regulation urgently required changing at the highest possible level. The Air Corps are under the illusion that they own the choppers when it is obvious that all defence equipment is state property. Therefore., there is a very strong case for transferring at least two of their 5 'Dauphin' helicopters to the naval service for continuous operational use aboard the vessel that was build to carry them. The navy could also train their own personnel to fly the 'Dauphins'. Later that year (1984), the *Satanta A15* was sold as scrap. She had proved to be of little use to the service and was almost worn out when they purchased her, and proved to be a very bad investment. That same year, the sweeper *Banba* was decommissioned and removed from service. Three years later, *Fola* and *Grainne* were also sold to a Spanish company for scrap for £90,000 for the three.

Now, the Naval Service possessed no vessels for inshore patrolling, and replacement ships for that purpose were urgently required. After much persuasion and coaxing, the government was finally convinced that vessels capable of inshore patrolling to help eliminate the illegal importation of arms and ammunition, plus the deadly cargoes of drugs, which are still being landed in increasing numbers around our unprotected coastline. Two ships of the Peacock class, which were being operated by the Royal Navy in Hong Kong waters became available, and were purchased by our government in 1988 for the rock bottom price of £4m each, and then sailed back by RN crews to Rosyth in Scotland, from where two crews from our service collected them and returned to Cork harbour in November of that year, with the *HMS Swift*, and *HMS Swallow* renamed *LE Orla P41* and *LE Ciara P42*, the prefix LE meaning Long Éireannach, or Irish ship. All our naval ships are named after women, famous in Irish mythology. The Peacock class had been constructed at the Hall Russell dockyard in Aberdeen between 1984-1985, at a cost of £10m each. They were Peacock, Plover, Starling, Swift, and Swallow. The Peacocks are excellent ships, being designed and constructed as proper naval vessels. Our navy are pleased that:

(1) They are capable of operating and covering 2500 nautical miles without refuelling at their economical speed.
(2) They have a maximum speed of 25 knots.
(3) The ships possess a built in watertight compartment system that enables the ships to stay afloat despite being damaged.
(4) The Peacocks are fairly well armed, with 1-76 mm Oto Malara guns, 47.62 mm general purpose machine guns, plus two 12.7 mm heavy machine guns added by our Naval Service when we took delivery.
(5) They have a displacement of approximately 690 tons.

Despite possessing a fleet of seven ships that are operated more efficiently than any other navy (all ships are at sea for at least 180 days each year), the service is still grossly undermanned and understrength to effectively police such a huge area of 132,000 square miles of sea. To allow for running repairs, refits, crew leave, and changing, we would require at least double that amount of vessels with three additional bases in Galway, Donegal and Dublin, to help maximise the service's efficiency in the fight against drugs that are killing our children and destroying our country, and to protect the EC Community fisheries. Despite the fact that the service remains grossly understrength, I am delighted with its progress. Since I left its ranks, over thirty years ago it has changed beyond recognition:

(1) The ships are of the highest quality, and are updated at regular intervals.
(2) Living conditions and food are also of the highest possible standards.
(3) Recruits, on enlisting, now possess a higher educational standard than the officers did while I served.
(4) Our ships servicing and repair facilities in Haulbowline contain the most technically advanced machinery and computers in the world.

(5) Our vessels now visit ports in Europe at least once a year. They have also paid goodwill voyages to North America, patrolled the waters off Canada, visited Bermuda and the Middle East on several occasions delivering vital equipment to our peacekeeping troops serving there.

The Irish Naval Service is thankfully no longer the laughing stock of the world, and it has indeed come a long way in the first fifty years of its existence.

The First Director of the Naval Service

After the war ended in 1945, the Marine Service ships were either scrapped or sold off, and its manpower drastically reduced from 300 officers and men to a ridiculous figure of one hundred and sixty three, all ranks. None of the remaining officers possessed any knowledge of naval training because they were former merchant marine personnel. In a Department of Defence memorandum, from the government headed Director of the Naval Service, it stated that:

(1) On 15th March 1946, the government decided that the Marine Service and the Marine Inscription should be retained as permanent components of the defence forces. As a result of this decision, one senior officer in the rank of Captain, and two senior officers in the rank of Commander will be required in the reorganised service.

(2) Officers holding such appointments should be men who are in possession of up-do-date knowledge of naval warfare, organisation, administration, and Naval Service conditions. They should be also capable of repairing and carrying out schemes of training, designed to meet the naval requirements of this country. It is considered that the best source of the supply of such officers is the British Navy, and that the appointment of a senior officer in the rank of Captain should first be proceeded with, and his advice then sought as to the officers to be selected for the remaining

two posts. The three appointments will be of about five years' duration.

(3) As a result of correspondence with a view to obtaining a suitable officer for appointment in the rank of captain, the British admiralty authorities, through the High Commissioner for Ireland in London, suggested that an officer whose services in the British Navy had already been completed, might meet the requirements of the Irish Naval Service, and in this connection, they furnished the names of two officers aged 46, who had retired in 1945, with the rank of Commander, and either of whom, in their opinion would prove suitable.

(4) From particulars supplied by the admiralty authorities, it appears to the Minister that Commander HJAS Jerome DSO would prove to be the more suitable officer. As a result of a subsequent visit of about one weeks' duration to Dublin for the purpose of an interview, Commander Jerome is considered to be eminently suitable for the appointment as Director of the Naval Service, in the rank of Captain. He has intimated his willingness to accept the appointment.

(5) The minister accordingly recommends that the government should advise the President to appoint to temporary commissioned rank in Oglaigh na hÉireann, Annraoi Jeroim (Henry Joseph Alexander Saville Jerome) in the rank of Captain marine rank with effect from the 1st December 1946.

What the above failed to mention was that Jake Jerome was in fact born in America, and that his father went to school in Ireland, two important facts that would have greatly increased his chances with the government of the day after the hatred directed towards us from Britain for our neutral stand during World War Two. Captain Jerome's term as Director was later extended for a further five years, but as I stated earlier, in this narrative, what was particularly noticeable during parade ground inspection when all personnel of all ranks were assembled he took great pleasure in shouting and screaming at his junior officers, using their surnames instead of the proper military fashion of addressing them by their ranks. This outrageous display was of course listened to and watched by the rank and file and everybody else present. This rank was only equivalent to that of an army colonel. Commander Tommy Thomas McKenna, another Merchant Marine officer, who served his time aboard tramp steamers, was commander of the base from 1946-1956, and was appointed Director after Jake Jerome finally retired, and most unfortunately, he continued Jake's disgraceful behaviour on the square.

A New Departure

Some important events and changes have taken place since I published this memoir in 1996. The most recent and disturbing development was the disposing of the service's first custom-built ship the *Deirdre*, which was at one stage the Navy's flagship, and pride and joy. She was disposed of at public auction at Haulbowline for the knockdown price of £180,000 plus auctioneer's fees, to a company which intends using her as a cruise ship in the Mediterranean. Following approval of the sale by the Defence Minister, the *Deirdre* was despatched to the nearby Cork Dockyard to be stripped of large sections of her superstructure and of her crew's living quarters. Then, on Wednesday October 24th 2001 at 7 p.m. she departed Cork Harbour for the last time, heading for warmer waters. She was accompanied by the farewell greetings of the whistles and sirens of most of the remaining sister-ships of the flotilla which she had proudly sailed alongside, covering 449,631 nautical miles, or the equivalent of twenty circum-navigations of the world since she was commissioned as a State ship in 1972. Therefore, she has certainly earned her keep and paid her expenses and running costs many times over. After her construction at the Verolme Dockyard in Cork she was described by many as a floating hotel, comparing her to some of the cruise ships then in operation, and well ahead of her time, with the added comfort of single and double cabin accommodation for the personnel on board. Her galley and the food it produced were of the highest quality. Her first crew were especially delighted and proud that they were chosen to operate this magnificent craft which was outstanding in all respects compared to the ex-British Ton class Minesweepers that had sailed alongside her. She will be forever remembered for her overall control in the capture and arrest of the *M.V. Claudia* off the coast of Waterford in November 1972, when the I.R.A. were attempting to land five tons of arms and explosives to kill fellow-Irishmen, women and children.

I also recall her part in the search and rescue attempts during the severe gale that affected the Fastnet Yacht Race in August 1979, when fifteen weekend sailors lost their lives and twenty-three of their tiny yachts were abandoned after losing their masts and their means of navigation, when their vessels' rudders were swept away by the force of the raging seas.

The *Deirdre* found and protected seventeen yachts in difficulty, and provided aid and assistance to a number of others after they were removed from the sea, and from their crippled pleasure-boats. Many of their crews swore that they would never go to sea again because of the frightening experience they endured when they were positive they were about to be lost forever.

Over her thirty-year life she has been lovingly cared for and maintained to the highest possible standards, and updated at regular intervals with the latest computerised technology. Changes were also necessary to install sound-proofing to eliminate high noise levels produced by her engine rooms, and a major overhaul was necessary only a few years ago to renew part of her hull, which was corroded due to the intake of water which had leaked through faulty portholes and accumulated behind bulkheads.

Because the *Deirdre* was of a new design, and the first of her kind, faults or 'snags' were bound to occur, and the first major flaw was the problem of shipping far too much water onto the bow as she pitched into the sea, frequently resulting in the bridge being engulfed in water, thereby shorting the electrical system and immobilising the bridge's equipment. A breakwater was installed on the bow, which finally eliminated the problem. Some alterations were also required to accommodate female members ashore in the naval base and aboard ship.

The newer vessels had female quarters incorporated into their original designs. Women are now fully integrated into all branches of the Defence Forces, and it has called for some major adjustments in style and work practices in a former male-dominated organisation worldwide over thousands of years. Many other navies in Europe, including Belgium, Norway, Sweden, Denmark, and Holland allow women to serve on sea-going vessels, and the French are fully committed to permitting women to sail on all their ships when their accommodation has been modified. In Latin America women serve in the navies of Venezuela, Brazil and Colombia. Peru and Chile only allow them to serve ashore in administration. In our naval service women undertake all duties in every branch ashore and afloat, and while at sea in all weathers, operating a twenty-four hour watch-keeping system on normal three-week patrols. When major problems frequently occur many servicemen have referred to this situation as being in a minefield without a map, not knowing what to say or do, while confined to very close quarters with the opposite sex for fear of being reported for sexual harassment to the officer in charge, and then being brought before the Captain for punishment.

One retired C.O. of a Dublin army barracks confessed to me that while he was in command the vast majority of cases brought before him were proved to be untrue, and that no sexual harassment incidents involving male members of the forces were reported to him, and that the majority of general complaints, 'cribs' were minor, and originated from female soldiers of all ranks. Furthermore, a recent report, written by a retired army captain for a thesis suggested that 60% of all female members of the forces complained that they were bullied. There were problems adjusting to this new situation, which was introduced by legislation in the Dáil in 1979 to enable women to serve in the permanent defence forces. This claim has been angrily dismissed and challenged by the male rank-and-file of all three services. So what constitutes bullying? Does it mean that when a group of new recruits ('red-arses') enlist in the forces, who are mammy's boys and girls, or wimps, don't want to take orders, don't want to learn the drill, won't or cannot do their duty, are sloppy and dirty in and out of uniform, a danger to themselves handling firearms and live ammunition, and who will not obey Defence Forces Regulations, should, and must get a bollocking, and if those weaklings refer to that as bullying they have absolutely no case to answer. Fully-trained personnel who will respond to orders immediately without question will always be an efficient team under pressure in emergency situations, and will, without doubt, save their own lives and the lives of their colleagues. So the bollocking on the Square will be their most valuable weapon at their disposal at the end of the day, and those fools who are claiming that they are being bullied really mean they are getting a bollocking, and more than likely they deserved it. Prince Andrew, the son of the Queen of England, received a severe bollocking on the parade ground when he enlisted in the Royal Marines, then cried in the ranks, and immediately ran home to his mother. Is that what we desire to defend our country, and those in war situations, where our young men and women serve throughout the world? Speaking for myself, I would obviously prefer a fully-trained and fit person defending me, rather than a wimp, male or female, who would run away afraid, and hide under enemy fire.

Despite the claims and counter-claims, I must admit that I have missed the golden opportunity to serve alongside, and socialise with the lovely young women now serving in the naval service ashore and afloat, not to mention the equally beautiful new ships.

When I served in the Navy we had nothing but horrible old ships, terrible food and living conditions, hardly any money, with dirt and ignorance thrown in. Now they have it all, including the female crew members, plus great pay, foreign voyages, TVs and videos, and mobile 'phones to check up on the women ashore, but most importantly a new public image that recognises them as professional and equal partners, participating in an enlarged protection force throughout Europe, apart from protecting our own sea area comprising 132,000 square miles of sea, four times the size of the island of Ireland.

However, the *Deirdre* was sold for a song, and has been re-named *Tosca IV*, a famous female name from an Italian opera according to Lieutenant Terry Cummins Slua Muirí, our operatic expert. As I write, the *Deirdre* is in an East German shipyard being modernised and refitted throughout to accommodate high-paying passengers to cruise and enjoy themselves in the warm Mediterranean waters, where she will end her days semi-retired, far away from the cold and grey Atlantic Ocean around our west coast.

The new vessel selected to replace her cost the State £22 million, and has been named *L.E. Róisín P51*. She was constructed at the Appledore Shipyard in Devon, England, and commissioned into our Navy in December 1999. She is magnificent in every respect, and a credit to her designers and to our service. This offshore vessel is seventy-nine metres long and is fitted with the most sophisticated computerised equipment available. She can steam at twenty-three knots, and travel 6,000 nautical miles without refuelling. *Róisín's* main armament is the Oto-Malera 76 M.M. dual-purpose fully-automatic gun which is in widespread use in many navies throughout the world, and this is also the main armament on our two coastal patrol vessels, the *Orla* and *Ciara*. This weapon is fired by remote control, with a rate of fire of eighty-five rounds per minute, at a maximum effective range of seventeen thousand four hundred yards. Although the *Róisín* did undergo extensive sea trials off the Cornish coast before she was handed over, but just two months later, in February 2000, while on patrol in heavy weather almost two hundred miles beyond our west coast, The Róisín suffered severe damage to her interior, including her dining areas, accommodation, and to her superstructure. One of her four bilge keel fittings which are attached to her hull to improve stability was whipped off by the raging seas. Something more important which could have proved fatal for the crew and the survival of the vessel was that her rudder was also almost lost, for when she was dry-docked in the old Verolme Dockyard it was discovered with horror that her only means of steering was being held in place by two small loose bolts. Since the *Róisín* was under full guarantee, a team of engineers from the Devon Shipyard were quickly despatched to Cork to rectify these serious defects, which resulted in the ship being out of commission for some considerable time, despite official denials, which stated that she continued to be fully operational and carrying out her normal functions. Far more stringent sea trials, tests, manoeuvres, and so forth, in all weathers off the coast of Cornwall in England would obviously have revealed the flaws in the *Róisín's* construction, without having to risk the crew and the ship in our severe Atlantic Winter weather.

One year later, in February 2001, her sister-ship, *L.E. Niamh P52*, the latest addition to the flotilla, was launched at the same shipyard in Devon ahead of schedule, and was finally commissioned into operational service by the Tánaiste, Mary Harney, in September 2001 at the Custom House Quay in Cork. The Navy now has in its possession eight beautiful ships, the largest flotilla in its fifty-five-year history. But despite its huge advancement in several areas it has had to cope with some sad and traumatic events during recent years, with the deaths of crew-members, while at sea. Leading Seaman, Michael Quinn, lost his life while attempting to save Spanish fishermen from the sea near Berehaven, Co. Cork in 1990. His friend and fellow crew-member, Able Seaman Paul Kellett, who was also attached to the *Deirdre,* received The Distinguished Service Medal with merit. Michael Quinn's medal was awarded posthumously.

Able mech. Robbie Dean from Cork was lost overboard in the vicinity of Newfoundland while the Navy's flagship the *Eithne* was steaming home after a five-week tour of duty in the United States where they had visited the ports of Boston and New York, and participated in The Tall Ships' Race on July 22nd, 2000. A.B. Dean failed to report for the four-to-eight watch in the engine room after a row had taken place in one of the ship's cabins while the vessel was nine hundred miles from the Irish coast. The body of 20-year-old Robbie Dean was never recovered. The crew of the *Eithne* relived their nightmare in April 2001 when another death in suspicious circumstances took place while the ship was alongside Dublin's south city quay. The body of the missing seaman, 22-year-old Brian Gorey from Limerick was recovered from the River

Liffey after a late Saturday night party had taken place aboard the ship. As I write the circumstances of his death are continuing to be investigated, but most unfortunately the Naval Service ships are acquiring a nasty reputation as places to visit while in port for late-night duty-free drink. There have also been cases of crew members being charged and reprimanded for drinking while on duty.

Far more serious cases of proven drug abuse and drug dealing throughout the service have also been severely dealt with by senior officers, and the courts. Shortly after the above incident on the *Eithne*, another crew member aboard an inshore vessel vanished over the side while no witnesses were present as the craft approached the entrance to Cork Harbour following a successful courtesy visit to Kiel in Germany, leaving all his personal belongings including presents, carefully packaged for transporting ashore. Investigation results revealed that no crew member attached to the ship could offer any explanation for his action. The Petty Officer's body was never recovered, despite an intensive search by all available vessels over several days.

Throughout history life at sea has always been difficult, highly dangerous and stressful, especially when young sailors were away from their wives and children for long periods of time, without any means of communication. But as I have already stated, today's seagoing personnel have access to instant contact with their families, loved ones or friends, who can reassure them that everything is in order while they are away carrying out their duties. Living and general conditions throughout the service couldn't possibly be better, so what's happening, what has caused the recent nightmares and unhappiness within the ranks, if pay and living conditions are excellent aboard State ships?

I know that stress and unhappiness is being caused by the presence of attractive young women working at close quarters on board ships of 200 feet long, on three-week patrols, twenty-four hours every day. I am also aware that human nature, being as it is, jealousy which affects both males and females is bound to have a serious effect throughout the entire crew, and that problems will, without doubt, continue while the vessels are crewed with young healthy members of the opposite sex. The use of hard and soft drugs has corroded and destroyed part of our population, especially our youth, since they are freely available within their places of entertainment. This is known to the Defence Department. Therefore, more frequent and comprehensive spot-checks must urgently be introduced to permanently remove that cancer, as it's quite clearly seriously interfering with their responsibilities and their judgements, which will at some stage endanger their ship and its crew in critical situations. The excessive consumption of alcohol while the ships are alongside or at sea must be tackled as a matter of urgency, since that also is obviously contributing to the Service's problems. Much stricter controls must be placed on the consignments of duty-free alcohol that each ship is issued with, as it commences its patrols. A far tighter system of distribution to each crew-member would ensure that no drink is consumed at sea, on or off duty, including within their living and sleeping accommodation, and that their minimum allocation of alcohol is strictly only consumed at official functions, and at meals, while the vessels are at anchor, or moored alongside. Drugs and alcohol must not be allowed aboard our State ships for personal use, and to eliminate that curse, which is destroying the Service's personnel and the Service itself, crew members returning from shore leave must be checked at the gangway by senior deck personnel, and those found in possession of drugs of any form must continue to be dealt with very severely. I must state very clearly that I retain the highest regard for the Navy and its personnel, and I do not wish to restrict in any way their enjoyment or quality of life within the service, but the complaints I have made are valid, and I am quite positive that if they are implemented the Service's image and functions will greatly improve and its personnel will operate in a more happy and professional environment in the future.

The shameful situation concerning the Naval Services Helicopter Carrying Ship the *Eithne P31*, has finally ended. On pages 170 and 171 of this book I stated that the *Eithne* was designed and constructed at a cost of £28,000,000 which was paid for by the tax-payers to facilitate the operating, repairs, refuelling, and to provide accommodation for the helicopter crews while serving aboard that ship. But despite this hugely expensive project, which was planned to greatly extend the area of patrolling and surveillance, whereby the aircraft operating from the naval vessel would cover a wider area on its mission, and report back on any unusual or suspicious circumstances, which could be investigated by the patrol vessel, whose personnel would board and search ships and arrest offenders. But these Government decisions didn't suit the Air Corps, who presented every excuse possible not to deploy the choppers aboard the *Eithne* for surveillance operations. But when they did agree, which was very seldom, they joined the ship in the mornings after breakfast in Baldonnell, when the vessel, would normally be operating on a three-week patrol, perhaps 200 miles off the coast, and then land on the after deck, have dinner, and later a short flight around the ship's patrol zone, followed by a return journey to Baldonnell, and home for tea, leaving the mother ship to proceed alone for the duration of her voyage. However, this farcical arrangement has at last been eliminated, and the *Eithne*, the only one of its class in the Navy, has closed down and sealed all systems connected with the operations of aircraft using her facilities aboard, such as landing and taking off procedures and maintenance, including refuelling and storing of helicopters, on the after deck and hanger of the *Eithne*, which is a loss to the country, and to the prestige of the Navy, who should be supplied with their own aircraft and pilots for operational purposes, and not depending on another service, whose main function in life seems to be transporting Government Ministers to official functions.

This year, 2002, commenced with a shattering blow to the Service when Warrant Officer John Lucey was tragically killed in a freak accident after falling from a height of 1,500 feet while hill-walking in a location overlooking Lough Duff, approximately three miles south of Carrantuohill, and eighteen miles from Killarney, County Kerry on Sunday January 12th. John was the General Secretary of P.D.F.O.R.R.A., the Permanent Defence Forces other Ranks Representative Association, a highly-organised and efficient body, which represents all defence force personnel below officer rank. John will always be remembered for his campaign, as one of the driving forces, along with Michael Martin, another Naval Service Warrant Officer, in the establishment of P.D.F.O.R.R.A. John's determination, efficiency, courage and intelligence was a contributing factor towards the improved pay and working conditions within all branches of the Defence Forces, and he is sadly missed by all his friends especially in the Naval Service.

On Sunday afternoon, February 10th, 2002 the newest naval vessel, *L.E. Niamh P52*, departed from the naval base in Haulbowline in a severe gale to commence a 25,000 mile round voyage to China, visiting Malta for refuelling, then sailing through the Suez Canal, heading to Eritrea to deliver vital supplies to our army peacekeepers serving there. She steamed to Singapore, then on to Hong Kong, where she arrived in time for the Saint Patrick's Day celebrations. The Minister for Defence Mr. Michael Smith TD the Chief of Staff of the Defence Forces, and the Director of the Navy, Commodore John J. Kavanagh, who is retiring this year, all arrived by plane to enjoy the festivities aboard the £22 million State ship, along with over one hundred Hong Kong based Irish citizens. The vessel visited the Far East to raise an awareness of Ireland in that region, which is being conducted by Enterprise Ireland, who have consulted with over two thousand Asian business leaders and seventy Irish businesses towards promoting Ireland's interests during the various visits aboard the *Niamh* continued her Asian trip to Shanghai, Cochin, Tokyo, South Korea, Penjang and Malaysia. During this historical voyage they presented paintings by Philip Gray, a former Naval Service Petty Officer who produced the excellent illustration in pastel for the cover of this book in 1996.

The Captain of the *Niamh* is Lieutenant-Commander Gerry O'Flynn, a fine officer from Courtmacsherry, Co. Cork, home of the famous lifeboat, and the ship's Navigational Officer is Roberta O'Brien, a twenty-four-year-old from the Glen of Aherlow, Co. Tipperary. I served with her grandfather, Chief Petty Officer Paddles McKeown in the Navy, and he is mentioned throughout this book, along with a photograph of him, which I published on page 122. I know that he would be so proud if he were still alive to see his lovely granddaughter as a Naval Officer on the Service's latest hi-tech vessel, navigating the ship on a round trip to the Far East, sailing 25,000 miles over a period of three months.

I feel that I must mention an important coincidence between the above historical voyage and the publication of this book. On pages 6 and 7, I have stated that the night before enlisting in the Service I was dreaming of life on the ocean wave, rushing from one foreign port to another, which included Bermuda, Miami, the China Seas and Japan, plus New York and San Francisco. Unfortunately for me I never managed to visit any foreign country during my tour of duty. But I am extremely proud that our modern Navy has done so. They have paid courtesy visits to Bermuda, New York, China and Japan, and I hope some day to be informed that permission has been granted to despatch an Irish Naval Service vessel to Miami and sunny San Francisco to fulfill my life's dream.

A callcard issued by Telecom Eireann
to celebrate the 50th anniversary
of the Naval Service in 1996.

An Slua Muirí
(The Sluggies)

The Naval Service's second line defence force was established in 1947 when its name was changed from the Maritime Inscription which had been formed, along with the Marine Service, the Naval Service's predecessor, and equipped with some barely sea-worthy junk, to defend Ireland against Hitler's battle-ships and ocean-going U-Boats during the so-called Emergency, from 1939-1945. Since 1947 An Slua Muirí (The Sluggies), has been responsible for the harbour defences of our four main harbours of Dublin, Cork, Limerick and Waterford, but in reality they have never been capable of undertaking that function, simply because they do not possess the training, equipment, manpower, or the proper vessels. For their No. 1 and No. 2 Company, stationed in Dublin, they are in command of a two-masted ketch the *Creidne,* which is normally moored in Dun Laoghaire, but is, at the time of writing, at the naval base in Co. Cork having a new diesel engine fitted. The No. 3 Company, based at Waterford operate a half-decker motor launch, a former diving boat, the *Freya,* which has undergone a major overhaul to her entire hull. No. 4 Company of An Slua Muirí, based in Crosshaven, possessed the *Nancy Bet,* a sail trainer of 21.5 tons, but she too was damaged, and sold off to a concern in Dublin. The *Nancy Bet* was replaced recently by the *Áine Laoi,* also a half-decker, and is in perfect condition.

The Slua in Limerick operate the *Barbara Heck* which was constructed in Youghal without an engine fitted, but a second-hand one was finally tracked down after being recently removed from an English fire-brigade machine. It was purchased and fitted to the *Barbara* Heck, but proved to be a terrible choice, since it has caused endless trouble, and proved to be quite unsuitable. Major repairs were also recently carried out to this boat's mast and entire electrical system at great expense. The above are all unarmed punts and sailing vessels, and would be laughable, ridiculous and absolutely useless in a crisis, bad weather, or a war situation.

I have enjoyed close contact with many of the 400 officers and men of the Slua over the past several years in the Naval Association, and I can state quite categorically that they are the most willing and enthusiastic group of men in uniform, awaiting the call of duty which they are more than willing to perform, but they do require much more intensive naval training to crew our highly technical patrol vessels as equal partners in the Regular Navy. Twice weekly they attend various army barracks across the country in full uniforms, similar to the regular naval dress, for lectures and naval training covering all branches of the Service, ashore and afloat. Unfortunately, since the Slua's establishment, the repetitive classroom instructions covering all those years since 1947 has, up to quite recently, not been put into practical use except aboard their sail training vessels or their inshore punts. Their only contact with our naval patrol vessels would be a social gathering in the ships' messes, perhaps after a military parade while The Navy would be visiting the Slua's local port, or while a presentation would be taking place. Every Summer each company travels to their beloved two weeks' annual training (holiday) in Fort Camden in Cork Harbour, close to Crosshaven, where they let it all hang out, and where it was a case of lock up your daughters securely while the Sluggies were on the rampage. This outing was eagerly awaited by all officers and men. Women have now, thank God (according to themselves) joined the Sluggies' ranks. When they bedded down at the old British Fort, which was constructed to safeguard the harbour, the Slua's biggest treat of all was, apart from the Cork young one's around the area, a day trip on a naval vessel which would simply involve a journey not much further than the open sea just beyond the mouth of the magnificent harbour. But here comes the hardest part of their ordeal. The naval ship would steam from Haulbowline, anchor, or simply heave-to and wait for their passengers the Sluggies, who were forced to row across the long journey from Camden in heavy sea-going whalers, and were very often exhausted and seasick when they reached the vessel and then they were compelled to climb aboard by a ladder netting that was secured to the side of the ship. That was more than enough for the young and most enthusiastic sailors who had been shackled to ancient and abandoned British Army barracks surrounded by green uniforms, parade grounds, and military equipment which they had absolutely no interest in, except their side-arms and general-purpose weapons which the Sluggies would be obliged to fire on the army ranges as part of their general training.

Of course, when the innocent part-timers happily crossed the decks of the ships the regulars took full advantage of the situation, offering to help them aboard and escort them to their messes and accommodation, using this golden opportunity to replace lost, stolen, or badly soiled items of valuable kit with lovely new and lovingly cared-for personal belongings which had been issued to, and signed for by the unsuspecting Sluggies. Therefore, at the end of the voyage the unfortunate Slua passengers were often too seasick, and simply in no position to inspect their kit-bag to ensure that everything was in order, and each of them only discovered that his immaculate uniform and other items of kit were now only a heap of shit, badly soiled with oil and grease from the boiler and engine rooms, plus paint and thinners, diesel and paraffin oil. He would be therefore compelled to replace the entire outfit on his return to barracks after his expensive cruise aboard a State ship. Strangely though, the regulars regarded this advantage taking as fair play, and justified their actions, which also included brewing-up tea with water removed from the ship's main boilers which contained a variety of water-softeners and chemicals, along with an assortment of oils and greases that enter the system from pumps and motors which drive the steam and water around the ship. The regulars always maintained that the part-timers needed to learn the hard way, and that they were civvies in real life, therefore they could well afford to pay to renew their kits. It's certainly a weird excuse for stealing another Serviceman's belongings, but that's how they justified their actions, when they were earning around £3 per week, with very little food, filthy conditions and horrible steam-driven ships.

As I have already stated they always have been a fine body of men, dedicated and proud to undertake whatever duty they were ordered to do. Today, thankfully, their position has greatly changed for the better, since the Sluggies, males and females together, may, if they desire, participate in complete patrols aboard the eight new ultra-modern vessels which are, as already stated, designed and fitted with special accommodation for the young Sluggie ladies, who thoroughly enjoy the sea, sand, sunshine and whatever else aboard ship. I'm not going to enter into any more detail in case their mothers may be reading this, and possibly identifying their lovely darling daughters. However, the technical training and techniques they gratefully receive will stand to them for the future, since the Slua is now part of the expanding Reserve Defence Force, who will be required to be fully trained and capable of integrating immediately with full-time regular defence personnel in the not-too-distant European Security Force, capable of defending themselves in a war situation. So their future will be bright, and much appreciated and assured. Over the years the Sluggies have been compared to the F.C.A., since both services are part-time operators, and are the right arms of their respective brothers, the regulars. But thankfully they have not been subjected to the vicious and hurtful name-calling that the unfortunate F.C.A. have had to endure over very many years, such as the 'Free Clothes Association', 'Fools carrying Arms' , 'Faggots carrying Arms' and, more recently, 'Sandbags'.

However, the Sluggies fellow part-timers operate roughly a similar rank structure, whereby all ranks, including officers, are attained through the system after first receiving their basic military training as recruits, square-bashing around the parade ground. One young F.C.A. officer who, having grown tired of serving in a green bull's wool uniform, decided that the naval outfit was smarter and more to his liking, and besides, he fancied himself as a naval officer and having a spell at sea on the ships and in the naval base's officers mess amongst his peers. However, when he transferred and joined the Navy's part-timers, he found to his disgust that the Navy's dress did not include a combat jacket that he looked so well in, and felt comfortable wearing. So, to solve this minor problem he simply declined to hand in his beloved F.C.A. tunic, and delivered it to the nearest laundry to be dyed navy-blue, and wore it throughout his long career until he retired as the highest Slua Muirí officer rank of Lieutenant-Commander, equivalent to Commandant in the F.C.A., which is also the highest rank to be obtained there. This gentleman was a highly respected officer who had come from a well-to-do family, but he, like us all in the two Services, had his peculiar habits. One was that he was very conscious that one of his ears was larger than the other, and that it tended to flap about as he marched around the Square and the various barracks. So, to eliminate that annoyance he simply ordered his caps to be two sizes larger than required, then tucked in the offending ear under the cap along with a chunk of hair. It was also well established throughout the Sluggies and the F.C.A. that he was very tight with money, 'as tight as a duck's arse, and that's water-tight', a former sluggie recently revealed to me. 'Yes,' he confessed, 'he always carried a little purse with him, just like a miser, and that's a dead giveaway, to identifying a queer, since real macho men don't wear make-up, deodorants, or carry purses. His reputation for meanness soon spread to the naval base, and when this Senior Officer had completed an extended annual training course he was issued with a larger than usual pay cheque. So a Senior

Regular Officer jokingly ordered a large group of Slua Ratings to immediately escort and safeguard the Lieutenant-Commander to the nearest bank to lodge his money in case he was tempted to spend part of it along the way.

Another Slua Senior Officer confessed to his colleagues that he derived his fullest enjoyment from sitting all day along the hills close to Fort Camden throughout his entire annual training, scanning the local beaches, coves, and inlets, looking for unsuspecting young females undressing or lying completely naked on the rocks or strands sunbathing, using the strongest binoculars available, and that he incorporated this holiday with pay into his annual holidays. He was always so concealed that the Company under his command frequently found it extremely difficult to locate him while they were stationed there. Ah yes, they were almost as wild and mischievious as we were across in Haulbowline or aboard ship. But the escapades of Neville Brennan and Mick McCarney who were leading seamen are still being recalled. Brennan is now a retired Chief Petty Officer, and McCarney a retired Petty Officer, and I can only relate one important incident, since they would probably be very embarrassed if I were to reveal all to the general public. One evening when both arrived in Fort Camden for annual training, McCarney was ordered by the Duty Officer to take over as duty Petty officer, to guard the fortress and secure the gate, which also involves ensuring that nobody must enter or leave without proper permission.

Anyway, Brennan and McCarney were determined to leave the Fort that night, on or off duty, since they had both been corresponding with two young local ladies throughout the year, having met them and fallen in love the previous year. All avenues were discussed with several of their colleagues as to how McCarney could be smuggled through the main gate without being noticed, for they feared that McCarney might crack up if he was forced to undertake his guard duty and miss the opportunity of meeting his sweetheart. Finally a plan was hatched whereby McCarney would lie flat under a roof-rack attached to Brennan's motor car, covered with a sheet of tarpaulin, and when Brennan was challenged at the gate by the fool who McCarney was supposed to relieve for the night, Brennan explained that the luggage on the roof of the car was a set of drums to play in a local band. However, both met their girlfriends, and much later, they foolishly entered a bar which was full of their colleagues, including officers who were aware that McCarney was supposed to be guarding the Fort that night. Both then panicked and drove quickly back to base, crossed the moat, entered a small door which was only known to a few, walked through a tunnel under the fortification into their accommodation, and straight into bed, assuming that they had fooled the entire Company. The following morning however, after breakfast Brennan and McCarney were marched up before the C.O., who was so outraged that he ordered them both to be dismissed from training for that year with loss of pay, and be sent home immediately. They slept that night outside the Fort in Brennan's car, and on Monday they appealed to the C.O. for a 'redress of wrongs', accompanied by Lieutenant Flannery, who was a self-appointed expert on fortification, who assured the C.O. that nobody could enter or leave Fort Camden except by the main gate. After much arguments they were allowed to continue their training.

Before concluding I will relate one more incident. A young newly-promoted Slua officer was so delighted and excited at the prospect of visiting the Officers' Mess in Haulbowline for the first time that he invited his lady friend to accompany him to show her off in the naval base, but as he approached Ringaskiddy and the road linking Haulbowline to the mainland he lost concentration and control of his car, and drove into a large hole left behind by the County Council. While sick with embarrassment and impending disaster, his vehicle was finally dragged from its deep grave by a squad of new recruits from the nearby base, who then escorted the officer and gentleman, and his lady friend to the Officers' Mess.

Naval Service Ranks and their Equivalent Army Ranks

Army	*Naval Service*
Lieutenant General	None
Major General	None
Brigadier General	Commodore
Colonel	Captain
Lieutenant Colonel	Commander
Commandant	Lt-Commander
Captain	Lieutenant
Lieutenant	Sub-Lieutenant
2nd Lieutenant	Ensign
Battalion Sergeant Major	Warrant Officer
Staff and Battalion Quartermaster Sergeant	Senior Chief Petty Officer
Company Sergeant	Chief Petty Officer
Company Quartermaster Sergeant	Senior Petty Officer
Sergeant	Petty Officer
Corporal	Leading Seaman (LS)
Private 3 Star	Able Bodied Seaman (AB)
Private 2 Star	Ordinary Seaman (Rating)